COMPARATIVE ECONOMIC PLANNING

COMPARATIVE ECONOMIC PLANNING

Edited with an introduction by
MARVIN E. ROZEN
THE PENNSYLVANIA STATE UNIVERSITY

D. C. HEATH AND COMPANY · BOSTON

Library of Congress Catalog Card Number: 67-26496

PRINTED SEPTEMBER 1967

CONTENTS

I. THE CASE FOR PLANNING

II. WESTERN PLANNING

III. SOVIET-AREA PLANNING

IV. DEVELOPING AREA PLANNING

DOUGLAS S. PAUUW

RAYMOND VERNON

V. QUANTITATIVE ECONOMIC PLANNING

BERT G. HICKMAN

INTRODUCTION

The evolution of national economic planning from an issue of recondite economic theory and bitter ideological controversy to a routine exercise of respectable economic policy is certainly one of the major intellectual themes of our time. What was allegedly theoretically impossible, because either the absence of private property precluded rational economic calculation in principle or the "millions of equations" could not be solved in practice, is now hum-drum work in chancelleries the world over. What was supposedly a matter of sharp and unbridgable division between warring social classes has become in large degree a question of pragmatic compromise and thus a job for the technician rather than the ideologue. This is not to say that strife over income distribution and deep social antagonisms have suddenly miraculously vanished from this world; rather, conflict resolution usually occurs within a planning framework.

The Emergence of Planning

Many powerful trends over the past three or four decades have contributed to the emergence of national planning. The Great Collapse of the 'thirties offered eloquent testimony to the instability of unregulated capitalism, and the rise of Keynesian thought provided an intellectual basis for short-run reformist intervention. The progress of planning in Soviet-area countries — recent troubles notwithstanding — has invited emulation. Continuing rapid advances in economic analysis and in data-processing facilities have established a framework for more extended and effective planning, and widespread concern for economic growth and development has led to increased planning as a vehicle for their achievement. Thus hardly an eyebrow is raised when that citadel of capitalism, the United States, imposes upon a developing country, as a condition of receiving aid, the requirement of national planning on the assumption that such aid will therefore be more wisely used.

But if planning is the wave of the future now present, we must still look more closely at the disparate reality which a common word obscures. There are immense and significant differences in approaches to planning, and it should not surprise us that the same word covers an amazing variety of practices. National plans differ widely in their comprehensiveness, mechanisms of implementation and enforcement, and objectives. Yet, there are great similarities in the techniques they employ: their use of economic models, their estimation and projective procedures, and their methods of solution. One of the purposes of this volume is to exhibit such differences as well as to reveal broad similarities.

Differences in planning practices reflect many considerations. Because continuity with the past somehow always asserts itself, a country's history and institutional framework affect its "style" of planning. Planning invariably involves considerable intervention into activities previously undirected, which explains why it sometimes proceeds so gingerly and at other times entails a major social revolution. Vital interests of important social groups are directly affected; this is not likely to meet with indifference and unconcern. Inevitably, planning poses many means–ends dilemmas, and the balancing of private claims against community goals. Who is to interpret community goals, what are the limits of the coercive powers of the state, how much heed is paid to due process and legality, how are the interests of competing groups reconciled? Clearly the answer to these questions cannot be the same everywhere but must reflect local tradition and institutional circumstance.

Similarly, there will be tremendous variation in all the requisites of planning. Staff and administrative scarcities, the capacities of implementing agencies, popular support, the degree and form of private cooperation — all will differ, so that the ability to plan would vary even if the will were everywhere the same. Furthermore, planning is beset with sufficient uncertainty and complexity to make it unlikely to become a rote and mechanical process, as the selections in this volume so clearly reveal. Planning problems will differ from country to country. For instance, what might be appropriate for a large continental country little dependent upon foreign trade may be singularly inappropriate for a small country closely tied to the world economy. Finally, it should not be forgotten that political and social goals will be inextricably bound up with economic objectives, and the character of these goals will be manifest in the form and content of national planning.

With respect to similarities, it is quite clear that the major influence is the neutrality of planning techniques. An input-output table does not pay much attention to political slogans; the universality of science is at work. In fact, as planning sheds more of its ideological origins, it is plausible that resemblances among various plans will increase. In the West, planning is being extended; in the East, it is being greatly modified; in the Developing Areas, greater realism and sense of proportion are becoming more pronounced. And as with most ideas, absorption takes place within the framework of local peculiarity thus producing exotic blends of old and new. Further, there is the trend towards internationalization of planning. True, in the past planning did suffer from a tendency toward insularity because of the illusory assumption that closed economy permitted greater control. Increasing dissatisfaction, however, with the results of this bias toward autarchy and an increasing realization that closed national planning is inconsistent with international interdependence have led to a reconsideration of this attitude. There is growing recognition that national planning must be tempered by international awareness and efforts at international coordination.

One final caution about similarities and differences needs to be strongly stated: namely, the need to distinguish appearance from reality. Planning has often been merely a sham activity and a public relations exercise. It is, after all, very easy to draw up a paper plan with no thought of how it is to be implemented, or to devise a plan which depends upon some *deus ex machina,* such as huge amounts of foreign aid or wildly improbable productivity gains, for its fulfillment. Frequently, what on paper seem to be immense differences or great similarities can turn out very much the other way in practice.

Planning Issues in Different Areas

Turning to the specific planning problems confronting each of the major types of national system — Western, Soviet, and Developing Areas — reveals more about the issues sketched above. In the West, planning has entered what may be termed its "post-full employment" phase. Not that the problems of maintaining full employment and whatever other goals might be specified along with it can be ignored; obviously they require continuous surveillance and action. Rather, other and broader ends now also demand and are getting consideration. The issues may be conveniently divided into three categories.

First, there are the "tidying up" problems: improving the quality of human resources, maintaining desired growth rates, ending regional development disparities, eliminating persistent pockets of poverty, dealing with urbanization difficulties, and facing such issues as environmental pollution, integrated transport systems, training and educational policy, recreational amenities, etc. Problems like these typically cannot be resolved by reliance on market mechanisms alone. Their complexity reflects the high degree of social interaction and interdependence characteristic of advanced and technically mature societies. Highly organized and articulate interest groups aggressively push forward their respective claims. In this milieu, planning tends to search for areas of consensus to bridge this diversity.

Incomes policies (or in their U. S. version, wage–price guidelines) are a second major planning issue in almost all Western countries. Persistent inflationary pressure seems to be the twin of full employment, and therefore stability always seems in danger. Incomes policy, in its various forms, is an effort to keep the struggle over relative income shares from triggering an unacceptable rate of price increase through wage- and price-affecting measures of differing severity and kind. Needless to say, this is easier said than done. Proposals range from elaborate formulae for sharing productivity gains over time to full-dress price- and wage-setting tribunals to *ad hoc* interposition of public representation in crucial wage–price decisions. For the most part, incomes policies have relied more heavily on exhortation than on more stringent forms of policy. Sometimes they have been substituted for a more intensive monetary and fiscal policy. Most economists, it is fair to say, have strong reservations about the efficacy of reliance on voluntary exhortation in this sphere; most policy-makers find their use irresistible for political reasons.

Finally, the nature and extent of planning itself is a matter of continuing controversy in almost all Western countries. The respective roles of persuasion and coercion; the relation between reliance on the market and central direction; the use of physical or financial, direct or indirect controls; the extent and importance of the nationalized sector; the use of incidental intervention or systematic guidance — all of these issues reflect the existence of basic political divisions within most Western countries. Thus they tend to be resolved on a country-by-country, case-by-case basis through the workings of the political process.

The dominant motif of Soviet-type planning is the state of flux which seems to characterize current efforts. The Soviet area is in a transition period. The dominance of the command economy, simple physical planning, the use of crude indicators, and devotion to excessive centralization all seem to be slowly eroding. What will take their place remains to be seen.

As the structure of Soviet society and economy evolved, it became increasingly clear that existing planning procedures were cumbersome, inflexible, and progressively obsolete. Periodic efforts at reform failed to come to grips with the critical planning issues. Evidence of inadequacy was manifest in a slowdown in the growth rate, and recurrent planning crises which necessitated *ad hoc* intervention. At the micro-level, numerous indications of inefficiency could be seen: high ratios of inventories to output, the existence of large unsold stocks of consumer goods because of shoddy manufacture or inattention to consumer preferences, the chronic tendency of decision-making units to extend their control over inputs to assure continuity of supply, and the bias against innovation because the rewards for risk-taking were small relative to the costs of failure. And above all loomed the spectre of planning procedures so complicated that the economy would be literally drowned in a sea of paper (and magnetic tape) of its own making. As the late V. S. Nemchinov, a prominent Soviet economist, said some years ago, "Should the old planning methods be preserved, and given our present rate of growth, in 1980 practically the entire adult population of our country would have to be engaged in the administration and planning spheres."

The changes occurring throughout Eastern Europe are the response to these difficulties. Central to reform are efforts to decentralize decision-making, but decentralization raises problems in many areas. For one thing, it makes imperative transformation of the information and communications system so that transactors will have reliable data upon which to base their decisions. Obviously a properly functioning price system would be of invaluable assistance in this regard. For another, the whole pattern of incentives and reward will have to be recast to harness individual effort and risk-taking more closely to proportionate remuneration. Such significant changes, however, squarely join the issue of political power and its sharing. To move planning in these directions is not, at root, simply a matter of optimal technique, a grand exercise in systems analysis, but rather raises fundamental issues of planner control and responsibility. Is there a halfway house where sufficient measures of decentralization, guided by a more rational structure of prices and incentives, can be integrated into a system of ultimate centralized control, or are attempts to create such a system doomed to failure? Within the next decade, perhaps we will be in a better position to answer this question.

Planning in the Developing Areas is least subject to generalization since differences among countries are so great. These countries have turned to planning primarily as a technique for accelerating their economic growth. In part, they consider planning desirable as a result of the successful Soviet experience, which seems relevant to their own condition. Also, the desire to plan reflects the vaguely socialist (or perhaps anti-Western) orientation prevailing in many of these countries and the historical association between socialism and planning. But most of all it stems from the inadequacy of the private sector and the consequent assumption by the state of an enlarged role in a country's economic life. This great desire to plan is, however, not a sufficient condition for successful planning; the condition of underdevelopment affects the ability to plan. One of the major problems is to adapt planning techniques to the particular scarcities and environmental conditions which characterize the Developing Areas.

These countries, for the most part, fall between two stools. They cannot or will not employ the degree of coercion which marked early planning in the Soviet Union; neither do their economies have the institutional flexibility and responsiveness to policy instruments which exist in advanced Western economies. Planning in the Developing Areas has been characterized by extensive make-believe and wishful thinking. Some of this performed a useful role in coalescing national energies and thereby helping to build a modern state. Political instability, however, a chronic affliction, exacted its toll by making continuity impossible. The immediacy and urgency of present problems invariably relegated consideration of the future to a low order of priority. In trying to do too much, it is likely they accomplished less than they could.

Yet it would be premature to conclude that planning in the Developing Areas has been and must be completely wishful thinking. They must traverse their own learning curve. Over time the scarcities which so limit their options will be removed; political stability will increase. Thus the incentive and need to plan should remain strong; and the environment will be more favorable. It would be a strange irony if the inevitable deficiencies associated with planning in its infancy diminish hope and make planning difficult when at last conditions become more favorable.

PART ONE

THE CASE FOR PLANNING

P. N. ROSENSTEIN-RODAN

Planning within the Nation*

Professor Rosenstein-Rodan presents the underlying rationale for planning. On a theoretical level, he argues that planning should produce better results than sole reliance on the price mechanism, chiefly by providing more information and superior coordination. He also discusses some of the modern techniques of planning and their applications, emphasizing particularly the use of shadow prices.

DEFINITION: Planning is just another word for a consistent and co-ordinated economic policy articulating explicitly and specifically its means and objectives. According to the objectives it has in mind it can be more or less comprehensive. Governments pursuing a certain type of monetary fiscal and commercial policy and outlining the anticipated effects of that policy practice planning in part like Monsieur Jourdain who talked prose all his life. A mere general development

* From P. N. Rosenstein-Rodan, "Planning within the Nation," *Annals of Collective Economy*, Vol. XXXIV (1963), pp. 193–207. Reprinted by permission of *Annals of Collective Economy*.

strategy through "sound" or "reasonable" monetary and fiscal policies would constitute, however, incomplete and insufficient planning because it could not provide guidelines or principles for determining the amount, the composition and the timing of public investments, nor indicate specifically the system of incentives and disincentives needed to orient the private sectors amount and composition of investment. A specific vision which sectors should grow at what rate is needed. General principles of "sound" economic policy alone are ungrammatical prose. Progress in economic knowledge makes it possible to plan for more than the limited objective of stabilization (aggregative planning). It can achieve the wider objective of accelerating the rate of growth and at the same time realize specific social objectives (distribution of income between classes or regions). Programming in practice can at least sharply reduce if not completely avoid inconsistencies in economic policy.

2. *Why is planning necessary?* The free and unimpeded mechanism of market forces would lead to a maximum national income according to the liberal classical doctrine. Any conscious deliberate active economic policy designed to influence the amount and the composition of investment could not, according to this school, raise national income in the long run. It is our contention that the opposite is true, that an economic policy designed to influence the amount and composition of investment can raise the rate of economic growth and increase national income. In addition, it can also aim at realizing other desirable social objectives which market forces alone — even according to the liberal doctrine — could not achieve.

According to the "liberal" school maximization of national income would be achieved by the working of the mechanism of supply and demand on assumption of competitive conditions and of small changes per unit of time in four stages or "equilibria": (1) allocation of given stocks of consumers' goods (consumers' equilibrium), (2) allocation of production on assumption of given stock of equipment (machinery), land and labor (producers' equilibrium), (3) allocation of investment on assumption of given stock of labor, land and capital (investment equilibrium), (4) equilibrium between aggregate demand and supply (monetary equilibrium).

It is true that under perfect competition the price mechanism would work perfectly in the first stage, i.e., in allocation of given stocks of consumers' goods. It would work less perfectly, but still tolerably well in the second stage, when we replace the assumption of given stocks of consumers' goods by flows of supply of these goods from given stocks of producers' goods. The price mechanism does not work in this sense, however, when we drop the assumption of a given stock of producers' goods and assume that the amount of composition of investment is to be determined by market forces. A multitude of individual investment decisions does not lead to an optimum amount and composition of investments for six reasons:

(*a*) the individual investment decision depends not only on present but also on future anticipated price of the project's inputs and outputs. The market provides only knowledge of present but not of future prices. Even the present prices do not always signal the proper information; they only do that under perfect competition which excludes indivisibilities and externalities. But future prices are uncertain and unknown. The creation of "perfect" future markets for all commodities is inherently impossible; such markets are only possible for a fraction of commodities. Additional information, of a type which is not provided by the price mechanism but can be provided by programming, can substantially reduce the risk and uncertainty about future prices.

The lifetime of equipment is long (say ten years) so that the investors have to have foresight. That foresight is bound to be more imperfect than that of the buyer and seller of a product. The individual investor's risk may be higher than that confronting an over-all investment program. Reducing this risk — which is possible under programming — may make additional investment possible.

(*b*) the individual investment decision depends not only on present and anticipated prices of the projects inputs and outputs but also on real or assumed investment decisions of other investors.

(*c*) the investor maximizes the private not the social, net marginal product. External economies are not sufficiently accounted for. Complementarity of industries is so great that simultaneous inducement rather than hope for autonomous coincidence of investment is called for.

(*d*) because of the indivisibility (lumpiness) of capital large rather than small changes are involved. Yet the price-mechanism works perfectly only under the assumption of small changes. A path towards a long-run equilibrium may lead through points of short-term disequilibria. Those would make it impossible to reach the long-run equilibrium unless programming measures, i.e., interventions from outside the market forces, were to direct them there. The price mechanism can only optimize under conditions of continuous convexity. Yet neither theology nor technology shows that God created the world convexly downward throughout.

(*e*) capital markets though often well organized are notoriously imperfect markets, governed not only by prices but also by institutional or traditional rationing quotas.

(f) it must be finally recognized that the wage level is indeterminate under modern conditions. Only when the economy is composed of very small firms and when each firm's wage revision affects such an infinitesimally small proportion of total income (for instance, raising or lowering wages of 100 to 500 workers in an economy of 20 million workers or more when the wages of all the others remain constant) that income effects can be neglected and only substitute effects matter, would the wage level be determined by the equilibrium theory. When wage revisions are in practice synchronized and affect large proportions of the labor force income effects can no longer be assumed to be of a second order of smalls. Collective bargaining does not determine "equilibrium" or "optimal" wages (i.e., these which are compatible with maximizing) and information as well as persuasion based on the content of national programming should help to establish them. Relying optimistically on a countervailing power which keeps wages at a level conducive to growth and social progress is unwarranted. Market forces can only determine wages in an atomistic economy consisting of very small units, not in the world of today.

The "investment" theory is indeed the weakest link in the "liberal" theory.

It is finally recognized even by the strongest advocates of a free economy that an equilibrium between aggregate demand and aggregate supply (i.e., the dynamic monetary equilibrium) cannot itself be ensured by trusting to the automatic responses of a free economy. This task can only be discharged by a deliberate policy. Without an equilibrium of aggregate demand and aggregate supply, however, prices cease to be reliable parameters of choice since money is not "neutral" and the price mechanism breaks down.

The automatic responses of the market economy do not ensure an optimum allocation in two out of four markets. The practical question is therefore not whether but how and how much to plan.

3. *The aim of planning* is — generally speaking — to achieve an optimum use of means for the fulfillment of the society's economic and social objectives, or more specifically, to maximize consumption over a given planning period subject to the constraint of terminal conditions of capital stock to be left at the end of the period and possibly also of some specific consumption targets or other social or regional targets to be reached at the end of the period. However long the planning horizon (five, ten, or fifteen-year plans) decisions as to the future beyond the plan period must also be taken in the form of what capital

stock (equal amount of capital per head of population, or higher amount per head) should be left maintained at the end of the period.

4. *Objectives of planning.* Objectives of planning are determined by the society's scale of values (value judgments incorporated in a "social welfare function"). The economist is not any more competent in deciding on what these values should be than any other citizen. The function of the economist, however, is to reveal and to show explicitly the implications of policy decisons and also the conflicts between various objectives. If the implications and the effects of some policies are revealed and shown explicitly decisions may be modified since decision-takers are often unaware of all the consequences of their proposed actions. In the same way, incidentally, projections of aggregate individual investment plans may reveal information and knowledge to the investors which the price mechanism cannot convey and lead thereby automatically to their revision. The primary function of planning in a free society is to increase the flow of information thus correcting the imperfect "anatomy of market failures."

5. *How does planning supplement the market forces?* The conclusion of the preceding paragraphs 2 to 4 is that the dispersal of investment decisions does not optimize economic development because it provides insufficient information. "Rational allocation of resources presumes a substantial flow of information concerning price and income elasticities, production and transformation functions, interindustry relations as well as a mass of 'aggregative' data. In a decentralized market economy a certain amount of these data is at the immediate disposal of decision-makers, i.e., those who control firms. A good deal of information relevant to rational allocation, however, in particular data on interindustry relations and the probable behavior of various aggregate quantities, can only become available with a substantial amount of government participation."[1]

The first and primary purpose of planning is to make available additional information to decision-makers of a type which market forces cannot possibly provide. This information alone would reduce risk, change investment decisions in the direction of improving both the amount and the composition of investment. Even if neither direct instruments of planning (public investment) or indirect means (incentives and disincentives for private investment) were to be used, a purely "indicative" planning would improve the risks of economic operations. The additional information would carry in itself consid-

[1] E. S. Mason, "Some Aspects of the Strategy of Development Planning" (Paper presented at the United Nations Conference held in Geneva in February, 1963).

erable persuasion to invest more or differently. Apart from additional information as to the means, programming also provides further information and clarification as to the ends by revealing the implications, complications, and costs of some ends so that the decision-takers may modify their actions since they are in practice unaware of the consequences of their action. Programming in this sense fulfils an important democratic functon of clarifying the content of the society's objectives: it helps to reveal the social welfare function.

Improvement in knowledge obviously leads to better allocation in time and space. As to time, it provides a larger horizon; while attempting to look forward one can realize that what seems sensible in the short run would not be optimal in the long run. As to space, it may provide criteria about optimum (or at least better) location by systemizing the long-run effects of location and concentration. Regional development, urbanization problems, industrial zones, etc., are not normally well provided via the market mechanism. Programming can finally reduce the risk of unforeseen changes. It can avoid an economic Maginot Line which if pierced or if broken through leads to a collapse of the system or at any rate to great losses which can be sharply reduced. Programming can develop an economic defence in depth in the sense of alternative programs providing second and third best solutions when the first one proves to be unattainable.

6. *Scope of centralization and decentralization.*

(*a*) Dispersal versus delegation of investment decisions. The liberal doctrine relied on *dispersal* of investment decisions as a risk-reducing device. Dispersal of decisions fulfilled the delegation of powers by the Invisible Hand. Modern liberals properly distinguish, however, between *dispersal* and *delegation*:

... *dispersal* of decision-making power which I have pointed to as one of the guiding principles of the liberal philosophy is not the same thing as mere *delegation*. The distinction is, I think, important. If an army commander gives general orders to a divisional commander, he at the same time delegates to the latter the duty of giving more detailed orders to *his* subordinates; and it is universally agreed that it will not usually make for efficiency if the army commander then butts in to see exactly what those orders are and how they are carried out. But there is nothing in this to alter the fact that if the army commander's plan is wrong, the whole army comes to grief. The dispersal of economic judgment commended by the liberal philosophy meant something much more than this, it was not merely a device for promoting administrative efficiency, but a recipe for securing that all the eggs should not be in the same basket — that in this highly uncertain world the fortunes of a whole trade, or a whole area, should not depend on the foresight and the judgment of a single centre of decision.[2]

The risks of an error in foresight and judgment of a single centre of decision cannot be denied. It is wrong, however, to assume that the dispersal of decisions will necessarily reduce the total risk. That would only be true if all the investment decisions were independent of each other; in fact they depend on each other. Consequently instead of cancelling out errors, such dispersal of decisions is likely to have cumulative effects. This is notably the case as far as the amount and the broad composition of investment are concerned. The means to realize these targets, the managerial and administrative decisions, should be delegated and guided by the price-mechanism; but the basic decisions as to how much and in what sectors to invest need not be arrived at simply by a dispersal of individual investment decisions. Programming — i.e., an over-all economic policy — can influence and change these decisions.

(*b*) Where to draw the line between delegation and dispersal of investment decisions.

In general the greatest part of sector investment programs, like programs for agriculture, housing, public utilities, etc., is usually clearly indicated; priority criteria for a dividing line between accepted and rejected projects need only be detailed in the critical zone of marginal projects. Some general common-sense criteria can be applied in the analysis of projects, for instance, "is it below optimum size," "is it well located," "will it be well managed." The choice between one project or another within the same sector will be flexible, however, and may often depend on the "impression" and the confidence the entrepreneur inspires. More detailed criteria could be worked out, given sufficient staff, data, and time. If all the projects were to be evaluated in that way, however, only a small part of the necessary investment could be "approved": even in the United States only half of the current investment could be realized if it had to pass all the usual project analysis criteria. Decentralization is called for as far as the selection of one project rather than another *in the same sector* is concerned. Dispersal of decisions here should provide the practical solution. In practice, therefore, programming should determine priorities between sectors, while a large zone of indeterminateness has to be admitted for the determination of single projects within a sector. Delegation of decisions as to sectors and dispersal of decisions as to

[2] D. H. Robertson, "The Economic Outlook," reproduced in *Utility and All That*, London, 1952.

single projects composing a sector seem to be the appropriate rules of programming.

Sector decisions must therefore be taken at the centre which alone can sufficiently account for externalities and establish a production program consistent with the requirements of interindustry supplies. The planning office will necessarily have to rely on sector plans which have been worked out by other agencies which received from the centre a list of basic mutually compatible assumptions. The implementation of those decisions through a multitude of managerial and administrative measures will of course be delegated. There is a vast variety of degrees of centralization and decentralization in various countries. In general the countries of the Iron Curtain have tended in recent years towards more decentralization while those of the West and the underdeveloped countries tended towards a higher proportion of centralized decision-taking.

7. *Decision on the composition of investment.*

A development program must be spelled out in projects but it is not a mere sum or shopping list of projects. Single-project analysis cannot use criteria which should simply consider each project in turn, see whether it passes the test or whether it does not, and according to that include in it (or exclude it from) the program. The various projects comprising a development program are interrelated and reinforce each other. This balance depends on whether complementary activities have been planned on the required scale. It is therefore practically impossible to judge the soundness of any particular project without the knowledge of the whole program of which it is a part. A program approach, not a project approach, must determine the criteria of productive use of capital. Replacing one project by another — leaving the rest of the program unchanged — would frequently be non-optimal. A change in one project may require a reshuffling and changes in several other projects. Only in the heroically abstract model of "two goods only" is there one alternative. In a world of many goods a program will differ from its alternative by a composition which involves more than the change of one single project.

Each investment project's contribution to national income depends on what other investments have been, are being or will be realized. The complementarities of all investment projects is more than a mere "complication" of a simple pattern; it introduces a new set of determinants of optimum investment. A program approach must therefore logically precede the project analysis even if it is recognized that in every country three quarters or more of projects (many of them in the public sector) are of such obvious priority that almost any plan would include them.

The effects of an investment policy depend on the total pattern of change. The degree of complementarity of investment projects and the divergence of social from private marginal product will be greater in an underdeveloped than in a mature, crystallized, developed economy. In the latter the environment of a project often seems to change a great deal. By shaking a kaleidoscope a "completely different" pattern can be seen, yet over 90 per cent of the particles — the nucleus — do not move, while less than 10 per cent of the marginal particles change their position. In an underdeveloped economy the unchanged nucleus is much smaller, the change affects a much higher proportion of particles — so that the whole pattern of change must be examined to evaluate any part.[3] The effects of an investment project on national income are the project's social marginal productivity. If it were possible to measure the social marginal productivity directly, it would constitute automatically the priority criterion for projects. Social marginal productivity of projects is unknown, however, and can be only indirectly assessed. Theoretically the proportion of net value added directly and indirectly (i.e., taking into account additional investment opportunities created by the project) is the project's basic effect on national income. Ideally this should give the priority criterion which might enable the government to determine subsidies for higher priority projects which would otherwise be selected by individual investors. In practice, however, the margin of net value added directly *and indirectly* by each project is even more of an "empty box" than other cost elements. An exact determination of the indirect effects is not possible outside the framework of a whole development program.

8. *Shorthand method of evaluation: shadow prices.*

Market prices under perfect competition are a signalling device steering economic resources into their optimum allocation. Prices of factors of production reflect then their opportunity costs and should be equal to their marginal value productivity. Competition, however, and the investment market are imperfect in reality. Shadow prices of three factors of production must be used in the evaluation of an investment program instead of market prices. This is not the place to expound the full theory of the subject. An excellent and succinct presentation is available.[4] Three operational points only may be mentioned: (i) Shadow prices are equal to the opportunity costs. If there

---

[3] One of the many vicious circles characteristic of underdeveloped countries is the fact that they need an economic civil service for programming most, while they have it least.

[4] S. Chakravarty, *The Use of Shadow Prices in Programme Evaluation* (CENIS, M.I.T., Cambridge, 1961, India Project C/61-28).

were only two goods in existence, the cost of one good is equal to that of the second good foregone. (ii) If there are more than two goods it is not so simple to identify the opportunity costs. The shadow prices enable us in this case to measure them. In the terminology of programming they are the Lagrange multipliers of a constrained optimization problem. (iii) To solve a constrained optimization problem for many sectors is a very complex task. A good approximation can be obtained, however, by calculating the shadow prices of factors of production for a simple two sector model and to apply them for each of the many sectors. Shadow prices can be used, therefore, as a computational shorthand method for each project without having to solve each time the optimization problem for the investment program as a whole, of which the project is a part.

While an exact determination of the shadow prices is not always possible, operationally useful approximations (within a lower and an upper limit) can be calculated. They are indispensable for the elaboration of an investment program in underdeveloped countries.

Since conditions change in the course of development a time path of shadow prices has to be assumed for a long-run plan. This does not apply in the case of a short-term plan.

(a) *The shadow rate of interest.*

Capital should not be invested in a project if thereby the opportunity is foregone of investing in another more profitable project. Since capital markets are notoriously imperfect the shadow market rate of interest should, therefore, be used as a computational shorthand in order to rank projects. The lower limit of shadow rates of interest in underdeveloped countries is around 8–12 per cent, say, 10 per cent.

Using R.M. Solow's formula (as an approximation) the shadow rate of interest ρ is:

$$\rho = \frac{g}{\sigma_R + \dfrac{1-D}{D}\sigma_W}$$

where ρ is the rate of interest, g is the rate of growth, σ_R is the savings rate of the profit receivers, σ_W is the savings rate of the wage earners, and D is the share of profit income in total income.

We guess that in a "typical" underdeveloped country D varies between 50–35%, σ_R between 15–35%, and σ_W between 3–6%. Assuming a rate of growth (g) of 4.5%, D = 60%, $\sigma_R = 25\%$, and $\sigma_W = 6\%$. The rate of interest

$$\rho = \frac{4.5}{0.25 + \dfrac{1-0.6}{0.6} \times 0.06} = \frac{4.5}{0.29} \ 15.5\%.$$

If the rate of growth were 5%, the rate of interest would be 17.5%. If $D = 50\%$, $\sigma_R = 30\%$, $\sigma_W = 6\%$ and $g = 4.5$

$$\rho = \frac{4.5}{0.3 + \dfrac{1-0.5}{0.5} \times 0.06} = \frac{4.5}{0.36} = 12.5\%$$

for $g = 5\%$ $\rho = 13.9\%$.

No project should be included in the investment program which would not cover interest costs of, say, 10 per cent.

Private investors follow this rule in practice. No investment project is undertaken, if it does not promise a return of 15–20 per cent. Public investment projects, however, neglect in general shadow-pricing — with grave consequences of waste of capital. Faulty allocation leads to the selection of wrong projects, wrong technologies, wrong location, wrong pricing of the product — and to insufficient savings of public enterprises, which should contribute to the national capital formation.

Electric power may be used instead of numerous other examples. A shadow rate of interest of 10 per cent will in many cases lead to the substitution of thermal for hydroelectric projects, to a location of thermal projects nearer to the market than the often distant hydro-electric projects, and to higher tariffs for electric power. Where specific subsidies are justified, they should be granted from the general budget. It is wasteful and too costly to give them indiscriminately to those who need it and to those who do not need it through lower prices of electric power. Prices which do not reflect costs cause a direct waste of resources (via lost profits) and an indirect increased and continued waste by inducing the location of power-intensive industries in high-cost areas.

In general, shadow rates of interest will give a lower ranking to capital-intensive and long-gestation period projects.

(b) *The shadow rate of exchange.*

Foreign exchange must be considered as a specific factor of production in underdeveloped countries. Low price elasticities of exports and imports are the cause of a foreign exchange market which either works imperfectly or works at an excessive expense of income growth. The scarcity of foreign exchange should be reflected in a shadow rate of exchange which is higher than the market rate of exchange.[5] In various underdeveloped countries shadow rates of exchange can be estimated at 10–50 per cent above the market rate. They give a measuring rod for the need of import-savings and export-gaining. While it is still uneconomical to produce bananas on the North Pole, shadow rates of exchange indicate to what extent projects, which produce goods at costs higher than prices of equivalent imported goods, should be included in the national investment program.

(c) *The shadow rate of wages.*

Where there is open and disguised unemployment shadow rates of wages are markedly lower than the market rates.[6] Theoretically the shadow rate of wages (Lagrange multiplier) is zero in such cases. Operationally, however, an "incentive shadow rate of wages" is necessary in order to induce the unemployed to work and to take account of the fact that the families of the unemployed will not save all they gave their family members as support, once those found an occupation, but will increase their consumption. Many projects which would not meet the criteria of priority if market rates of wages were assumed, should nonetheless be included in the development program on the basis of shadow rates of wages which are 20–50 per cent lower than the market rates. These should be primarily labor-intensive projects which use little or no capital. An important example are rural public works (fencing, bunding, terracing digging for minor irrigation) which use little capital and increase the productivity of the land, although at first they do not produce an increase in agricultural goods. If the workers live in villages and work nearby a wage rate lower than the market rate might induce them to work. If they work away from their homes a market rate of wages might be paid and subsidies would be justified.

Shadow prices are not a substitute for but a derivation from a full development program. An oversimplified two-sector model of such a program can be constructed, however, and its results (shadow prices) can be then applied to a disaggregated many-sector model. This short-hand method is of special importance in underdeveloped countries where market prices differ from "equilibrium" prices to a larger extent than in developed countries.

[5] The use of an accounting price of foreign exchange is not necessarily a substitute for devaluation; it does not imply that devaluation is necessary.

[6] P. N. Rosenstein-Rodan, *Disguised Unemployment and Under-Employment in Agriculture* (CENIS, M.I.T., Cambridge, 1956, Italy Project C/56-25).

9. *The typical conflicts between objectives. Examples:*

Conflict between more consumption "today" and more consumption tomorrow.

Conflict between more employment "today" and more employment than would otherwise have been possible tomorrow.

Conflict between a higher rate of growth and more equal (personal or regional) income distribution.

etc., etc.

10. *Content of development plans.*

(*a*) *The means.* Any development program consists of two main parts:

A. "What is to be done?" (often outlined sketchily in a "Framework" (Schema for Development)

B. "How is it to be done?" (Implementation)

A alone is clearly insufficient. A coherent well coordinated economic policy must be used throughout as a purposeful instrument of growth. It will have to determine what part of investment is to be undertaken in the public sector (*direct means* of planning) and what part is to be undertaken in the private sector (influenced by the *indirect means* of planning). A system of incentives and disincentives apt to encourage or discourage private investment in certain sectors, regiona or technologies constitute the "indirect means."

Besides the means of monetary fiscal and commercial policies, national wage and income distribution policy must be planned and agreed upon since monetary and fiscal policies alone are insufficient to "determine" the wage level.

(*b*) *The planning horizon.* Any short-term plan can logically be only determined within the framework of a long-term plan. In practice very few decisions would have to be changed today in the light of what will happen twenty years later. A perspective plan for fifteen years seems practically to be the best logical basis. In a short-run plan many bottlenecks must be accepted as unavoidable which can be changed in a more flexible longer-run plan; they elaborate the short-term aspects of a long-run plan.

(*c*) *The degree of disaggregation.* A long-term (fifteen years) plan may be less disaggregated than a shorter-term plan. Even in a short term, planning should concern broad *sectors* and not the individual projects within those sectors. How much output is desirable from sectors can be decided by an over-all plan. The implementation of this decision to projects within sectors may be delegated (decentralized).

11. *Classification of plans.*

(*a*) Long-run, medium-run, and short-run plans.

(b) Global, sectoral and regional plans.

(c) Aggregative plans for limited objectives of:
   i stabilization (control of effective demand)
   ii equilibrium in the balance of payments (see f)
   iii full employment (planning for income distribution rather than growth)

(d) Limited disaggregation models.

Investment in social overhead capital as an impulse to induce (via the multiplier and acceleration mechanisms) spontaneous private investment.

(e) Disaggregated (multisectoral) intertemporal models are needed for:
   i mapping out alternative feasible paths of development (Consistency Models);
   ii selecting one of the feasible paths (Optimization Models). These models can be constructed in a way of explicitly focussing one or more policy decisions which have to be determined. They are called "Decision Models" by J. Tinbergen. According to the number of decisions to be determined there will be corresponding degrees of freedom in the model: the number of unknowns will exceed the number of equations by the number of decisions.

(f) Plans classified according to the proportion of direct and indirect instruments used:
   i Stabilization plans (c) i use exclusively indirect means. Balance of payments plans may use only indirect means. (c) ii or in addition some direct means (quotas import licences, exchange controls, etc.).
   ii Disaggregated models may use varying proportions of direct means (public investment, investment licensing, training programs, establishment of industrial estates, etc.) and indirect means (incentives and disincentives of credit-fiscal and commercial policy).
   iii Planning is purely *"indicative"* if no direct instruments are used. Apart from conveying information indicative planning may also rely on *persuasion* without using other means. Planning may be *"inducive"* if only indirect means (incentives and disincentives) are used. It may finally use direct and indirect means (as under (f) ii) without becoming *normative*.

12. *Experience of Planning Policies.* A separate detailed study would be required to describe the procedures and assess the results of planning policies in the last decade. In a detailed study, however, a

specific conclusion how much of the success is due to planning and how much to other coincidental measures is difficult to draw. This is not the place to provide such a survey, discussion, and analysis. All that can be said is that in all the developed countries at least the aggregative planning for purposes of stabilization and, if need be, balance of payments equilibrium have been applied and produced economic structures markedly different from those of the pre-war period. In addition, in all these countries 26–33 per cent of national income pass through or are determined by the public sector so that in this sense at any rate they are truly models of a mixed economy. Only aggregated measures of economic policy have been taken in the U.S. and not much more has been applied recently in Great Britain although preparation for a more disaggregated planning (NED) are currently in the offing. Holland based its economic policy on scientifically determined decision models, had a sensitive, careful, and successful aggregative plan (see 11 (c)) and had moreover a tripartite system of wage negotiation where government representatives participate in collective bargaining. It has not, however, applied disaggregative models trying to influence the allocation of investment among different industrial sectors. Italy had a limited disaggregated model underlying the development program for the south to which some more specifically disaggregated features were added after 1957. The ten-year development program for Italy as a whole (Vanoni Plan) was a framework for development rather than a plan (see 10 (a)A. but not B.) but it was more disaggregated than the plan for the south. Even without specific instruments of implementation it had at any rate some effects of persuasion to invest and provided rough elements which can add up to indicative planning. France applied indicative planning through the Monnet Plan and most economists believe that without it the present economic structure of France would not have been achieved. In addition to indicative planning, the Monnet Plan most successfully exercised persuasion on French investments and the credit policy of the French banking system reinforce this persuasion with better credit conditions for those investments which were agreed upon in the Plan.

In underdeveloped countries, India has put her economic development plans as the foremost objective of her national policy. The plan is based on a disaggregated inter-temporal model and an elaborate institutional setup is provided to study and revise the plan. Pakistan has a similar program although development does not seem to have the same top priority in its national ideology. In Latin America the Alliance for Progress has directly appealed for all member States to elaborate their development programs. Some of them, like Colombia and Chile, have already done so. Others (Mexico, Venezuela, Peru, Honduras) have prepared short-term plans which are to be followed quickly by more elaborate long-term plans.

The institutional implementations of various countries differ very much and the realization of the plans show varying differences between ex-ante projections and ex-post results. But the trend is throughout in the direction of disaggregated inter-temporal models as a basis for their development policy.

13. *Problems posed to democracy by planning.* The preceding reflections clearly show that planning does not endanger the main freedoms of a democratic society. By relying on the functions of providing additional information (indicative planning), persuasion, and largely indirect means of incentives or disincentives rather than on coercive measures, planning can improve the attainment of economic and social objectives, of a higher rate of growth, and social progress. By explaining the implications of alternative paths of economic policy it should mobilize an intelligent cooperation of the main economic sectors who will thereby become aware of the consequences of their action and of their social responsibility. The so-called private sector should finally realize that the rate of growth including economic benefits for the private sector have been on the whole better in the post-war decade where the government participation controlled from one-quarter to one-third of the national product. The antediluvian principle that "to govern better is to govern less" is definitely buried. Let us rejoin our century and our generation and realize that governments are not a necessary evil but an important and valuable complementary factor in production. We may conclude therefore that planning can preserve the main freedoms; far from endangering it may improve the functioning of a democratic society.

J. K. GALBRAITH

Development Planning
and Practice*

Professor Galbraith, in his usual witty manner, concentrates on planning in the context of the Developing Areas. His essay, by liberal use
of analogy and comparison, has wider application to planning in
general. For its wisdom and deftness it has been included in this
introductory section.

Not long after World War II, on a mountaintop in Switzer-
land, a group of somewhat aging and wholly perturbed scholars
gathered to survey the scene and consider what should be done about
all of the talk of planning and postwar planning then so much in
vogue. Many stories have been told of that gathering, most of them no
doubt apocryphal. One is of a bitter debate over whether to take a
stand, as a matter of principle, against the public ownership of naval
vessels. On this, some of the most spirited opponents of planning
were inclined to compromise. But the purists are held to have insisted
that naval defense should be supplied by private enterprise through
competitive bidding.

Whether this discussion took place or not, it should have, for it
contains all of the outstanding characteristics of the debate over planning: the tendency to see it as a religious issue, as a test of faith rather
than as a practical question of public policy; the tendency to see a
conflict between the market and planning, although prices can be a
very useful instrument of the planner; and the tendency, above all,
to identify public ownership and planning. All of this has been a
source of great confusion and, as a result of this and the curious tendency for all discussions of the subject to attract those who say the

* Reprinted by permission of the publishers from John Kenneth Galbraith
Economic Development, pp. 60–75, Cambridge, Mass.: Harvard University
Press, Copyright, 1962, 1964, by John Kenneth Galbraith.

17

most and know the least, most people, on encountering the word "planning," decide to read no further. In general they are well advised.

Planning by national communities consists, first, in establishing selected objectives or goals and, second, in devising a method or design for reaching them. In the last century, the emerging industrial communities of Europe and North America accepted pretty much whatever fortune the miracle of economic progress brought them. We can agree that they did no planning, although it could be argued that, in the early years of the American republic, Alexander Hamilton's *Report on Manufactures* was the forerunner of the modern plan. In modern times, however, all advanced national communities have established fairly firm goals for themselves in matters of economic policy and have devised measures of greater or less efficiency for seeking to reach these goals. All can thus be said to plan. The United States holds before itself the need to keep unemployment below a certain maximum and to sustain a certain level of accomplishment, in relation to that of the Soviets, in defense and space exploration. It is also disposed to set itself a certain percentage rate of growth of Gross National Product, but there has never been agreement on what it should be, and only economists remember the current rate. As the United States sets as its goals, in many matters, keeping ahead of the Soviet Union, so the Soviet Union sets as its goals catching up with the United States. In this aspect of planning, there is an excellent reciprocal relationship between the two countries. Each makes it impossible for the other to succeed too easily.

The difference between modern national communities is not in having a plan, but in the degree to which the existence of the plan is avowed, in the formality with which the goals are spelled out, and in the particular techniques used to achieve the goals of the plan. The United States, being officially an unplanned economy, does not avow its planning. It also uses techniques appropriate to its particular stage of development. India, Pakistan, Ceylon, are less reticent. And the techniques are the rather different ones that serve a much less advanced stage of development.

 I have elsewhere discussed the planning goal of the less developed country; it is the improvement of the well-being of the modal person. This goal is the counterpart of the poverty of the poor and it is not only central but total. Rich countries have the luxury of a choice of goals; poor countries do not. My concern now is not with the goals of planning but with the techniques for achieving them. Here we encounter two closely interrelated and much debated questions: first, the extent of state initiative, as opposed to market incentive, that is required for reaching planning goals; and second, the extent to which state initiative requires public ownership of productive facilities.

On one area of state initiative, there is general agreement. Where something must be brought into existence which cannot readily be bought or sold and which is deemed so important that it ought to be available to everyone, then a direct action by the state is necessary. Such, for example, is the case of education or the provision of roads or the prevention of disease.

There is implicit but not explicit agreement on another field. When, to go a little distance for a phrase, a great leap forward is necessary, there is no alternative to a state initiative. For the development of atomic energy in the advanced countries, there was no alternative to government action. Similarly with space exploration. The initial passages to the moon will cost some tens of billions of dollars. This will almost certainly discourage the average tourist and prevent the business from soon being placed on a paying basis. Accordingly, apart from the hideous possibility of remaining at home, there is no alternative to government-sponsored moon travel. The old-fashioned subsonic jet passenger transport would not have existed except as a by-product of government-sponsored military development. The development of supersonic transport has had to wait on government initiative. One rewarding result of these necessities has been the discovery of how much government initiative is welcomed in a capitalist economy once it is discovered that capitalism cannot do the job.

Where, however, no great leap is involved, there is a choice between having the initiative with central authority or leaving it to the market. In the United States the government on at least one occasion intervened to increase steel output. Rather more frequently, it has obtained more by leaving it to the market. Wheat production in the United States can be reduced — the problem of increasing output has long been academic — either by applying rigid controls or by allowing prices to fall in a sufficiently painful degree.

There is also some choice between whether the operating units in areas of state initiative — the organizations which provide roads and schools, the firms which organize the production of steel, atomic power, or supersonic aircraft — will be in public ownership or not. The traditional theory of planning has normally held that state leadership requires state ownership. Hence the ancient association between planning and socialism and, parenthetically, much of the suspicion aroused by the word planning among private enterprisers. In practice, however, there can no longer be said to be any rule. Public ownership of schools and roads is agreed. Elsewhere there is some difficulty in telling what public ownership really is. Thus, the United States, deferring to conservative dislike of socialism, has numerous private corporations which, however, sell only to the state. Their costs, prices, profits, and even executive salaries and expense accounts are subject to a measure of public restraint or review. The private ownership is largely nominal, although all concerned will insist on it, and some of the people involved are among our most vehement anti-socialists. And in some areas — research and development, atomic energy, electrical energy — the United States does make extensive use of public ownership.

By the same token, some countries make extensive use of private ownership of productive units even in areas of state initiative. In Poland and Yugoslavia, the state plays a role of considerable importance in relation to agriculture. But the industry remains substantially in private ownership.

The unplanned economy makes use of market incentives — higher or lower prices and incomes — to induce changes in output. The same device is almost equally pervasive under planning. The difference is not in the instrument but rather in the goals it serves. Thus, efficiency in the Soviet Union is rewarded by paying profits to executives and workers. Workers are encouraged to greater effort or to less agreeable jobs or localities by the promise of better pay. This is a very practical matter. There is no reason for having an individual do something badly or unwillingly by public order when he will do it well and willingly in the pursuit of personal reward. Similar procedures are followed in the other planned economies. Yugoslavia has made especially imaginative use of market incentives. The use of such incentives, like the use of public ownership in the Western economies, is still resisted in some degree for reasons of faith, but in diminishing degree. In all of the advanced economies, there is an increasingly pragmatic selection of instruments — state initiative, various forms of state ownership, market incentives — for reaching goals.

The underdeveloped, even more than the developed country, needs to know where it is going. The problem of progress is one of elementary prevention of hunger, exposure, disease. So here the existence of a plan is an imperative. This is agreed even by countries which conceal their own commitment to planning. As a result, for the developing country the word planning has ceased to be controversial. Five-year plans are the invention, and were once the exclusive possession, of the Soviet Union. Now Americans and Western Europeans with impeccable credentials assemble in consortiums presided over with unquestioned respectability by the World Bank to consider financing for the five-year plans of India or Pakistan. The country which does not have goals, and a program for reaching these goals, is commonly assumed to be going nowhere. This may well be so.

There are three further reasons why in the beginning stages of economic development, planning takes on special importance. A number of the steps that have the highest priority at this stage — education and improved transport and communication — are, by their nature, among the things which require the initiative of the state. Nineteenth century governments, though they could contentedly accept whatever the market provided in other areas, took the lead in providing popular education and in building railways, roads, canals, and communications systems. No country has ever obtained a satisfactory school or road system by leaving it to the private sector. Most railroad systems have an extensive history of state initiative and subsidy. Matters are still the same for the new country now.

Secondly, the new country, like the developed country, must use state initiative where a long leap is required. But in the new countries the leaps are not the exception. I have noted that, where the development of supersonic travel or communication by way of earth satellites is involved, the developed countries turn without hesitation (and without criticism except occasionally for the delay) to state initiative. These are *their* big leaps where the market cannot be relied upon. But in India the development of a steel industry, or a heavy engineering industry, or even a watch industry involves a comparable leap. Accordingly, it requires a comparable initiative by the state. The setting up of the huge Fairless works of the U.S. Steel Corporation near Trenton was a comparatively commonplace response to market prospects. The establishment of a plant of similar proportions at Bokaro in India, although there is little doubt about the demand for the steel, is a mammoth undertaking, and without state action nothing would happen. Only individuals with a uniquely simple approach to the problems of economic development, or a peculiarly determined ambition for conservative applause, will make the mistake of generalizing from market performance in the developed country to what the market can accomplish in the poor country. It is no part of the good fortune of the poor country that this larger state initiative is required. As I stress elsewhere, economic development imposes, generally speaking, the greatest burdens on those governments that are least able to bear them. This is not a happy arrangement of human affairs but unfortunately there is no sign that such affairs were arranged for maximum convenience.

Finally, the poor country is under a particular compulsion to conserve resources. Not only is capital scarce but some of it comes free, or at concessional rates, as aid from abroad. Left to the market and the local distribution of income and demand, an undue amount would be invested in high-priced housing or the manufacture of expensive consumers' goods for the benefit of the well-to-do. And scarce resources in foreign exchange would slip away into luxury imports. All this is normal in the rich country but offensive in the poor. The United States in modern times has been the first to urge planning measures — licensing of luxury imports or taxation of luxury building — to prevent such waste. Conservative opponents of foreign aid are the first to complain when they hear about a recipient country importing Cadillacs.

Planning being peculiarly necessary in the poor country, I turn now to the requirements of a good plan. Of these, there seem to me to be four. And in present-day development planning, all are in some degree honored in the breach. The price of this neglect is considerable.

The first requirement is that the choice of instruments for the execution of the plan be pragmatic. In the developed countries, capitalist or communist, although the contest between the theologians and the practical men continues, the latter, as I have noted, are in the undoubted ascendency. In the United States, it is no longer necessary to find an appropriate doctrinal justification for a very extensive exercise of government initiative. One measure of the scope of this initiative is the proportion of the Gross National Product controlled and disposed of by the state. In the United States, this is approximately 20 percent of the total, as compared with 13 to 14 percent in India. There is similar pragmatism in the use of price and profit incentives across the Iron Curtain. Even British Socialists, in some ways the world's most ardent defenders of doctrine for the sake of doctrine, have largely given up on public ownership or have reduced their commitment to it to a purely symbolic level. That is because it no longer serves a clear purpose in the British economy. The common denominator of all this change is the tendency to accept, sometimes rather reluctantly, what works.

Nothing, I think, is more to be recommended to the less developed lands than the same salutary tendencies. And here, unlike the more industrialized countries East and West, the test of works, not faith, has still to make its way. China is far more purist in application of doctrine than the Soviet Union. Partly as a reflection of the high church rigor of British socialist doctrine, socialism *qua* socialism rather than what socialism accomplishes is still an objective of many of the former British territories. This means that the test of public or private ownership is not necessarily what best advances development. Rather, in some metaphysical sense, it is what advances a socialist pattern of society. As a result, economic performance is regularly sacrificed to doctrine. And the suggestion that a more pragmatic test would be wise is resisted with a good deal of moral indignation. One wing of the modern left prefers in practice to attack capitalism and accept poverty rather than have a greater measure of progress with a pragmatically mixed economy.

It is worth repeating once more, especially for the improvement of those who might take conservative comfort from this formulation, that a pragmatic course requires equally that public ownership be accepted where this is required. The test of what is practical works both ways.

The decision on other instruments should be equally pragmatic and here, also, there is room for improvement in the less developed lands. The purposeful use of price incentives and disincentives can be a major substitute for administrative effort and time. No one doubts that good prices to farmers — and it is wholly consistent with effective use of the price system that these be guaranteed by the state — are superior for increasing output to orders enforced by police and magistrates. But likewise high import prices, the result of high tariffs and realistic exchange rates, may be far more efficient than import licenses for rationing scarce foreign exchange. It may be wise to exclude luxuries by fiat. But ability and willingness to pay may not be a bad test of the effective use of capital goods imports. Similarly, high interest rates, testing again the need of the community for the investment, may be superior to a system of licenses and permissions as a device for rationing capital. High prices of imported capital or high interest rates may also usefully take the pressure off the planning system and thus play a useful supplementary role. The man who must pay the full price for imported goods has that much less incentive to offer bribes to obtain a license. Even where the price system works less precisely than a system of licenses, franchises, permissions, and orders, there may be a strong case for it because of its remarkable capacity for eliminating the costs of delay.

The second requirement of a good plan is that it be accommodated to the level of economic and cultural achievement of the country in question. In the beginning stages of development, plan creation is not properly a matter of economic planning at all; rather the goal is to build basic administrative organs, to develop the educational and basic cultural structure, and to get a viable and progressive social system. In Western Europe and the United States, following the

French and American Revolutions, these steps laid the foundation for economic advance. The same steps following the Meiji restoration laid the same groundwork in Japan. In developing its Central Asian republics, the Soviets gave high priority to developing an effective system of provincial administration, to education, to providing a transportation system, and to getting the nomads into a settled system of agriculture.

It follows that, in the early stages of development, the task is not to set production targets and plan investment outlays. Rather it is to lay the administrative, social, and educational groundwork for such investment. Only in later stages is detailed planning of investment in order. It belongs, relatively speaking, to a rather advanced state of development.

The third requirement of a good plan is a sense of strategy. This applies, particularly, to the fairly advanced countries just mentioned. The standard modern development plan is an investment plan. It reflects decisions on how best to employ scarce capital resources. Its primary goal is the thing that investment is assumed to accomplish, namely a specified and presumably adequate rate of economic growth. In this planning, a good deal of thought goes into the matching and phasing of the various segments of the plan — into insuring that kinds and amounts of steel being produced or imported will match requirements for steel in kind and amount, and that this balance between supply and requirements is maintained over time. Equally careful attention is accorded the supply of investment resources — the question of where, internally and externally, the capital is coming from. One can find little fault, in principle at least, with the way this part of the planning task is performed.

There is a grave danger, however, that such a plan will present all things as equally important. They are not. Some things are broadly catalytic in their role. Others are indispensable for improved well-being. Other things are merely passive and useful. A good plan must provide a strategy for economic advance. It is a well established fact that among angels virtue goes unnoticed. Equally if everything is held to be vital, the truly vital escapes attention.

By way of illustration, in an industrialized country a highly efficient transportation system and an economic and reliable source of power are indispensable. With these available, something is certain to happen; without them, one can be less sure. These industries provide the external economies of other industries. They make it possible for others to exist. In the somewhat different case of agriculture, while many things are useful, a few things are indispensable. Water, fertilizer, and improved seed can revolutionize agriculture. Other agricultural services, by contrast, have only a limited impact. Veterinary medicine, improved packaging, marketing advice, home economics may be useful but they will produce no major change.

Strong forces work against strategic concentration. In any country engaged in planning there is a relentless pressure on individuals, departments, and regions to have favorite enterprises included. To be outside the plan is to have a nasty sense of exclusion with practical financial consequences as well. The desire not to be accused of overlooking something is also strong. So there is a tendency for the plan to become not a plan but a list of all the things that should be done, that everyone would like to have done, or that anyone believes ought to be done or which might be a cause of criticism if overlooked. Specification of the things of strategic urgency is lost.

In the American colonies prior to independence and in the early years of the republic, there was no great surplus of food. The space between the mountains and the sea along the Atlantic was limited and not everywhere fertile; the demands for food and fodder sometimes exceeded its capacity and food had to be imported from Europe. A plan formulated along modern lines for relieving this situation would have emphasized the need for agricultural colleges, extension services, veterinary services, plant breeding, better marketing, control of insect pests, advanced horticulture, fish culture, and the provision of storage capacity for buffer stocks. Doubtless also there would have been mention of the need for improved transportation. But among all the other excellent and useful ideas, this could easily have been overlooked. In 1825, the State of New York opened a canal which connected the black lands of the West with the centers of population. On its completion, the food shortage came to an end and there has been no sign of recurrence. This canal was the strategic factor in the plan. The importance of isolating and emphasizing the elements of strategic importance is not less in the developing country today.

The fourth requirement of a good plan is that it emphasizes both the visible and the invisible dimensions of industrial achievement. Like an iceberg, much of a modern industrial society is out of sight. And, also like an iceberg, the invisible part has the greatest capacity for causing shipwreck. To get capital plant — railway lines, coal mines, airplanes, oil rigs — into use is the visible achievement of development planning. To ensure that this plant is efficiently used — that management is independent and sound, and that in consequence product quality is good, cost of production low, and earnings adequate for replacement and expansion of plant — is the much larger part of the task. This part lies below the surface. Nor is it sufficient that the developing country be only adequate in these respects. It must be more efficient than its older competitors. It was by low cost and efficient production that Germany and Japan won their places in the industrial constellation against the competition of the earlier arrivals. New industrial countries, such as Israel and Yugoslavia, have recently been making their bid in the same way. It is thus that both domestic and foreign earnings for further expansion are won.

I think it extremely important that the modern plan set firm targets, especially for publicly owned firms, for this invisible achievement. As valuable as firm targets for steel output are firm targets for man-hour productivity, costs, and returns. Goals so set become binding on all concerned. All are challenged to meet them. All have a sense of failure if there is a shortfall in performance. And there is, in addition, the highly practical fact that failure can be identified with those responsible. If there are no standards, then no one fails the examination. Promotion and honor accrue to all alike. Economic achievement was not meant to be that easy, and certainly not in a developing nation. Socialists are oddly reluctant to accept advice from non-socialists on what to believe. That is partly because they are so regularly advised to give up their belief in socialism. It may still be worth reminding all socialists, nonetheless, that the most damaging thing that has happened to the idea of public ownership is the growing belief, reinforced by numerous and visible practical examples, that it is shockingly inefficient.

In much of present planning, targets are set for visible physical accomplishment — for capacity in place or for production. This is the easiest and certainly the smallest part of the task. But targets are equally practical for managerial performance, labor productivity, costs and returns; all lend themselves admirably to objective measurement. It is of the greatest importance that the modern development plan be as complete in respect of these goals as any other.

PART TWO

WESTERN PLANNING

COUNCIL OF ECONOMIC ADVISERS

The Employment Act:
Twenty Years of
Policy Experience*

Twenty years of experience with the Employment Act of 1946 have provided the Council of Economic Advisers with a rich opportunity for review and reflection. In this selection, the Council analyzes how economic policy has met the challenges of those years and what problems still lie ahead. It emphasizes the necessity of flexibility to deal with the swiftly changing nature of our economic problems and the need for innovation to deal with new problems. The Committee's remarks on the desirability of having a well-informed and responsive public in order to carry out economic policy effectively within a democracy raise a vital issue, frequently overlooked.

* Reprinted from *The Annual Report of the Council of Economic Advisers,* pp. 170–186, January, 1966.

THERE WERE great expectations and not a few qualms when the Employment Act was signed into law on February 20, 1946, following enactment by heavy bipartisan majorities in both houses of Congress. This year, which marks the 20th anniversary of that enactment, is a suitable occasion to review our experience under the Act, to take stock of where we stand today, and to consider the challenges ahead.

THE ACT AND ITS BACKGROUND

The legislation of 1946 set forth the following declaration of policy:

> The Congress declares that it is the continuing policy and responsibility of the Federal Government to use all practicable means consistent with its needs and obligations and other essential considerations of national policy, with the assistance and cooperation of industry, agriculture, labor, and State and local governments, to coordinate and utilize all its plans, functions, and resources for the purpose of creating and maintaining, in a manner calculated to foster and promote free competitive enterprise and the general welfare, conditions under which there will be afforded useful employment opportunities, including self-employment, for those able, willing, and seeking to work, and to promote maximum employment, production, and purchasing power.

In making this declaration, the Congress recognized that the billions of independent spending and saving decisions of a free economy could well result in levels of total demand either short of full employment or in excess of productive capacity. Furthermore, it took the view that Government policies could play a constructive role in improving the stability and balance of the economy.

The Act was a product of the experiences of the Great Depression and World War II. The Depression shook but did not destroy the faith in an automatic tendency of the economy to find its proper level of operation. In the early 1930's, public works and other antidepression programs were justified as temporary "pump priming," to help the private economy get back on its track after an unusual and catastrophic derailment. And the departure from orthodox fiscal principles was made with regret and without complete consistency. The Government expenditures explicitly designed to combat depression necessarily increased budget deficits; but this implication was veiled by financing these outlays through an "extraordinary" budget. Meanwhile, taxes were raised, and salaries and housekeeping expenditures cut in the regular budget, thereby reducing the over-all stimulation of Government measures.

The relapse of the economy in 1937 into a sharp decline from a level far below full employment gave rise to conflicting interpretations. To some, it proved that pump priming and Government deficits had undermined the confidence of the business community and thereby only worsened the situation. Others, however, concluded that it pointed to the need for larger and more sustained fiscal and monetary actions to revive the economy. In drawing this conclusion, economists were buttressed by the writings of J. M. Keynes, who offered a theoretical explanation of the disastrous depression. The Keynesian conclusions received additional support during World War II because they offered a satisfactory explanation of why the high deficit-financed defense expenditures of that period not only wiped out unemployment but went beyond to create inflationary pressures.

Memories of the disastrous 1930's were very much in the public mind as World War II was drawing to an end. Many active proponents of "full employment" legislation in 1945 and 1946 feared a relapse into depressed levels of economic activity like those of the 1930's, once military spending ended. They looked toward Federal public works spending as a peacetime replacement — at least, in part — for the wartime defense outlays.

The opponents of "full employment" legislation had several reservations and objections. Some feared that it would mean a statutory blessing for perpetual budgetary deficits, soaring public expenditures, and massive redistribution of income from upper to lower income groups. There were doubts that Government actions could and would on balance raise employment; and there were fears that these actions would lead to regimentation and would jeopardize the free enterprise system. The proponents of legislation, on the other hand, argued that the Act would merely provide a setting essential to the proper functioning of the free enterprise system because a depressed economy heightened social tensions, discouraged innovation and initiative, dulled competition, and undermined confidence.

The legislation which finally emerged from this discussion wisely abstained from diagnosing depression as the disease and public works as the cure, but instead concentrated on establishing the principle of continuing Government responsibility to review and appraise economic developments, diagnose problems, and prescribe appropriate remedies. And it placed major responsibility squarely upon the President, who was asked to discuss his execution of that responsibility in an Economic Report to be transmitted to the Congress at the start of each year.

The Act also established two agencies — the Council of Economic

Advisers in the Executive Branch and the Joint Committee on the Economic Report (later named the Joint Economic Committee) of the Congress — with interrelated but separate responsibilities. These institutions have each filled a vital and previously missing role in their respective branches of Government — they have provided a coordinated overview of the economic impact of the entire spectrum of Government tax, expenditure, monetary, and other activities. To maintain the emphasis on advice and coordination, the Joint Economic Committee was not given any substantive legislative responsibility nor the Council any policy-executing duties. Both agencies have participated actively in the counsels of Government; both have conscientiously striven for a thoroughly professional economic competence and approach in their respective reports and recommendations; and both have contributed to the public understanding of economic issues.

Today's economic policies reflect the continuing impact of the Employment Act in all the years since its inception. And our accumulating experience is certain to be reflected in the policies of the future. This chapter reviews the development of policy in the past 20 years and outlines the present relationship between economic analysis and economic policy.

AVOIDING DEPRESSIONS AND BOOMS

The Congress proved wise in its decisions to state goals broadly and to concentrate on continuing review, analysis, and proposals, since the specific problems that actually arose were somewhat different from those which many supporters of the Employment Act had anticipated.

Although an important part of the impetus for the Employment Act derived from the prolonged depression of the 1930's and the resulting fear of stagnation in the American economy, this problem did not prove to be the primary challenge to economic policymaking under the Act. Indeed, immediately after World War II, excess-demand inflation proved to be the key problem. Subsequently, policy was focused on the age-old problem of limiting the size and duration of cyclical swings. Only much later and in a much different and milder form did stagnation arise as a live issue.

Thus, much of our experience under the Act consisted of policy actions to combat recession — lest it turn into depression — and to contain excess demand pressure — lest it generate inflationary boom.

Combating Recessions

A series of relatively short and mild recessions required Government attention in the postwar period. The problem of cyclical declines was not unexpected by the framers of the Employment Act, nor was it new to the American economy. In the period between 1854 (the beginning of the business cycle annals of the National Bureau of Economic Research) and World War II, we had experienced 21 periods of recession or depression. Our postwar record is blemished by 4 additional periods of contracting economic activity — 1948–49, 1953–54, 1957–58, and 1960–61.

Compared with the previous cyclical record, the postwar recessions have been far shorter, considerably milder, and substantially less frequent. Postwar recessions ranged in duration from 8 to 13 months; the average duration of previous declines had been 21 months, and only 3 had been shorter than 13 months in length. Measured by the decline in industrial production from peak to trough, postwar recessions ranged in magnitude from 8 percent to 14 percent. By comparison, in the interwar period, the declines ranged from 6 to 52 percent; three of the five contractions exceeded 30 percent and only one was less than the 14 percent maximum of the postwar period. During the past 20 years, the economy has spent a total of 42 months, or 18 percent of the time, in periods of recessions, far less than the 43 percent applicable to the 1854–1939 era.

Discretionary Policies. This improvement in the postwar record of the economy was aided by the deliberate discretionary steps taken by the Government to modify the impact of business downturns and thereby to prevent cumulating declines into depression. The speed and force of these actions — in both the fiscal and monetary areas — varied among the recessions. Thus, in 1949 little new fiscal action was taken, partly because inflation was viewed as a key problem even during the decline, and partly because Government measures taken the previous year were expected to have a considerable impact on the economy: the tax reductions of 1948 were supplying large refunds, and large expenditure increases were forthcoming under the recently enacted Marshall Plan. The Federal Reserve did act to reduce reserve requirements in a series of steps during the spring and summer of 1949, reversing a two-year rise in short-term interest rates.

In 1953–54, as military outlays declined and aggregate activity retreated, the principal expansionary influence came from previously scheduled reductions of corporate and personal income taxes. But some new action was taken to reduce excise taxes and to speed up expenditures. All three major instruments of monetary policy — reserve requirements, the discount rate, and open market operations — were used to encourage the expansion of credit-financed expenditures.

Meanwhile, the Administration planned larger fiscal steps that might be taken if the recession seemed likely to be prolonged. Significantly, in 1954, the bipartisan character of expansionary fiscal policies was established for the first time, as the Republican Administration of President Eisenhower adopted measures that had previously been linked to the New Deal and Keynesian economics.

In 1958, the recession was considerably deeper than its two post-war predecessors and both the Eisenhower Administration and the Congress were more vigorous in taking action. An important concern of earlier years — that business confidence might be disturbed by Government recognition of a recession — seemed insignificant since the sharp recession was obvious to all.

Several important measures were taken. The benefit period for unemployment compensation was temporarily extended. Grants to States under the Federal highway program were enlarged and accel-erated, and other programs in the budget also were expanded or rescheduled to provide an earlier stimulative effect. The Government also acted to spur housing activity by financial operations in the mort-gage market and by altering terms on Government-guaranteed home mortgages. The important measures were launched near, or after, the trough of the recession. Thus, in retrospect, policy helped most to strengthen the early recovery rather than to contain or shorten the recession. Nevertheless, in view of the general recognition that the Government would be running a substantial deficit in any case, these additions to Federal outlays were a significant reflection of changed attitudes toward the role of fiscal policy.

Monetary policy also played a constructive role in the 1957–58 recession, once the monetary authorities moved to ease credit 3 months after the peak in economic activity. Thereafter, Federal Reserve actions contributed to a revival in housing and other investment by promoting a sharp reduction in interest rates, both short- and long-term.

The first fiscal measures to deal with the 1960–61 recession were taken with the inauguration of President Kennedy in January 1961, when the recession had just about run its course. Nevertheless, improvements in the social insurance system, rescheduling of Federal expenditures, and expanded programs (including defense and space) were an important stimulus to the recovery during 1961. In contrast to the delay in taking fiscal measures, the Federal Reserve reversed a tight money policy early in 1960, prior to the downturn.

Not all discretionary changes in taxes or expenditures have contributed to economic stability. Indeed, some steps taken to pursue national security or social goals had destabilizing economic impacts, which were not always appropriately offset. Previously scheduled payroll tax increases took effect in 1954, 1959, and 1962, and drained off purchasing power in recession or in initial recovery. In 1953, defense outlays declined and triggered a recession before offsetting expansionary policies were adopted.

Structural Changes for Stability. On the whole, discretionary fiscal and monetary actions made a distinct positive contribution in limiting declines. Even more important in this respect was the strengthened inherent stability of the postwar economy.

In large measure, this can be traced simply to the greater size of the Government relative to the total economy: that is, the increased importance of Government expenditures — both purchases of goods and services and transfer payments. Government outlays do not participate in the downward spiral of recession; because of its borrowing capacity, the Federal Government — unlike businesses and households — can maintain its spending in the face of declining income receipts. Although State and local governments do not have equal immunity from the need to tighten their belts, they have been able to maintain their growing spending programs relatively unaffected during the mild postwar recessions.

The increased relative importance of Government outlays is shown in Chart 13. Social insurance and national defense have added especially to the post war totals of Federal outlays. State and local outlays have been rising rapidly in an effort to catch up with neglected needs and to keep up with the desires of a wealthier society for improved public services.

The contribution to the stability of the economy resulting from a high level of Government expenditures, insulated from revenue declines, has been augmented by the cushions to private purchasing power provided by the built-in fiscal stabilizers.

When private incomes and employment decline, purchasing power is automatically supported by both a decline of Federal revenues and an increase in unemployment compensation payments. Transmission of the virus of deflation is thus impeded. During postwar recessions, the progressive Federal personal income tax has not had to demonstrate its full stabilizing effectiveness because of the mildness of dips in personal earnings. There have, however, been sharp declines in corporate incomes; the Federal Treasury has shared about

Role of Federal and State and Local Governments in the Economy

PERCENT OF GNP

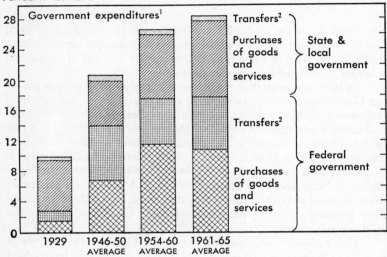

Government expenditures[1]

Transfers[2]

Purchases of goods and services

State & local government

Transfers[2]

Purchases of goods and services

Federal government

1929   1946-50 AVERAGE   1954-60 AVERAGE   1961-65 AVERAGE

[1] National income accounts basis.

[2] Transfer payments, net interest, and subsidies less current surplus of Government enterprises.

Source: Department of Commerce.

half of the drop in profits, thereby helping to bolster dividends and to cushion cash flow, and hence investment outlays.

A number of improvements in our financial structure were developed in the 1930's to assure that financial collapse and declines in economic activity would not generate a vicious downward spiral as they did after 1929. These important financial mechanisms include Federal insurance of private deposits; the separation of commercial and investment banking functions; the Federal Reserve's increased ability to provide banks with reserves in time of crisis; and the joint work of the Federal Reserve and the Securities and Exchange Commission to reduce harmful speculation in the stock market. The very existence of these structural changes has contributed to stability by improving confidence.

With the help of the more stable structure of the economy, recessions in the postwar era have been limited to declines in investment spending (and, in 1953–54, Federal outlays). Consumer incomes have not declined significantly, and hence households have maintained their spending in recession. With the nearly two-thirds of GNP represented by consumer expenditures insulated from decline and with a solid foundation of public outlays, declines in private investment have not cumulated. In contrast, the Great Depression generated a decline of consumer outlays of 40 percent from 1929 to 1933, and the shrinkage of consumer markets aggravated and reinforced the collapse in investment spending.

Containing Inflationary Pressures

The desirability of price stability was clearly recognized in the legislative discussion of the Employment Act. But few considered the danger of postwar inflation nearly as great as the opposite danger of relapse into depression. The legislation itself emphasized the objectives of using resources fully and attaining high employment. It did not explicitly label price stability an objective of policy, although this was implicit in the Act and fully reflected in the policies of every Administration. Nevertheless, concern has been expressed at times that policies for "maximum employment" might allow demand to press too hard on available resources, thus biasing the American economy toward inflation.

In the wartime environment, inflationary pressures of excess demand had been suppressed by direct controls on prices and by rationing. It turned out, however, during the years immediately following World War II that these measures had served partly to postpone — rather than to eliminate — significant demand pressures. Substantial backlogs of demand emerged in the 1946–48 period. Consumers and businesses possessed large accumulations of liquid assets to finance the rebuilding of their depleted stocks of household appliances, machinery, and equipment, and their houses and plants.

Thus, contrary to expectations, the initial years of the postwar era were marked by excessive rather than inadequate demand. In this environment, living standards of consumers, the productivity of labor, and the capacity of businesses rose rapidly. But so did the price level, with a jump of 31 percent in consumer prices from June 1946 to

August, 1948. Automatic fiscal stabilizers helped to contain the growth of private after-tax incomes, and were reflected in budgetary surpluses during the period. The economic policymaking machinery set up under the Employment Act may have moderated pressures to cut taxes drastically. Meanwhile, monetary policy was tied to a policy of supporting Government bond prices and was not free to combat inflation.

During the Korean war, however, the Government acted vigorously to counter inflationary tendencies close to their source. The March 1951 Federal Reserve-Treasury "accord" unleashed monetary policy. Selective controls on consumer instalment credit and on home mortgages were instituted. The enactment of three large increases in income and profits tax rates in 1950 and 1951 is one of the better examples of timely fiscal policy. These actions reflected, in part, recommendations by the Council of Economic Advisers and hearings and reports of the Joint Economic Committee.

Right after the outbreak of hostilities, prices had risen sharply in a flurry of consumer and business buying and, as a result, prices and wage ceilings had been imposed early in 1951. Once the restraining influence of over-all fiscal and monetary policies was fully felt, there was little pressure on the ceilings, and the economy was able to meet the peak defense demands of the emergency without inflationary strain.

The immediate postwar period and the early months of the Korean war are the two blemishes of clearly excessive demand on our postwar record. Apart from these two intervals, wholesale prices have shown a net increase of only 2 percent in the postwar era. In 1956 and 1957, the only other periods of marked price increases, over-all demand was not generally excessive. That inflation raised new issues, which are discussed below. In view of the whole postwar record, it can hardly be said that the Employment Act has biased policy toward inflation.

EVOLVING PROBLEMS AND POLICIES

During the postwar era, the American economy has remained free of the malignant diseases of depression and run-away inflation. And the rate of economic growth has considerably exceeded its long-term average. The objectives of the Employment Act, however, have not always been fully met. In particular, experience has demonstrated that the avoidance of depression did not guarantee the achievement of "maximum employment" and the avoidance of excess-demand booms did not assure the maintenance of price stability.

Inadequate Demand in Expansion

The strength of private demand in the early postwar years and then again immediately after the Korean war led to a reassessment of the tasks of stabilization policy. After a decade of postwar experience, suspicions arose that the typical problem would be to contain rather than to stimulate private demand.

Any such conclusion was soundly refuted by the facts of the ensuing years. With the backlogs met, and with a marked decline in the rate of family formation, private demand weakened in the late 1950's. The economy's performance weakened correspondingly because Government did not act to compensate. Thus, while unemployment had averaged 4.2 percent of the civilian labor force in the first postwar decade, it remained above that level every month between late 1957 and October 1965, averaging 5.7 percent.

The problem of inadequate demand in expansion, which became the primary focus of fiscal action in the 1960's, was a new challenge to policy-making under the Employment Act. In the first postwar decade, each time the economy advanced or rebounded from a recession, it reached the neighborhood of full employment. The policy-makers had been ready in the early postwar years to deal with noncyclical problems of submerged prosperity or stagnating production. They had seen maximum employment as a moving target which could be maintained only through a substantial growth of output. Both the Council of Economic Advisers and the Joint Economic Committee had given these issues repeated attention in the late 1940's and early 1950's. But until the late 1950's, no experience had been encountered to distinguish the problem of full employment from that of cyclical prosperity.

Then came a sequence of disturbing events: the 1957–58 recession followed a year of slow advance; the 1960–61 recession began from a peak far below full employment; and the expansion that began in 1961 seemed to be running out of steam after little more than a year.

During the initial years of this period, Government policy maintained vigilance against excessive buoyancy of demand when that was no longer the problem. Restrictive fiscal and monetary actions choked off the recovery of 1958–60. The shift to an expansionary fiscal policy by the Kennedy Administration early in 1961 was designed primarily to initiate a thriving recovery. A determined policy strategy to assure complete recovery was first formulated when the economy faltered in 1962.

The combination of fiscal stimuli to consumer demand and direct tax incentives to investment, together with monetary actions permitting an ample rise in credit, promoted a vigorous and sustained expansion after 1963. The inherent strength of both consumption and investment demand appeared in a new light, once the Revenue Act of 1964 exerted its invigorating influence.

Inflation at Less Than Full Employment

Another problem encountered at times during the postwar era has been the tendency of prices to rise even in the absence of over-all excess demand pressures. This tendency reflects structural characteristics of the American economy. The economy is not made up of fully competitive labor and product markets in which large numbers of buyers and sellers interact and respond passively to prices. On the contrary, in many industries both unions and businesses exercise a considerable degree of market power. As a first result, wages and prices are both somewhat rigid in a downward direction. To the extent that prices rise more readily in response to excess demand than they decline in the face of excess supply, the price level is given an upward bias, which can become particularly acute if there are sharp shifts in demand among various sectors of the economy. Secondly, because of market power, some firms augment increases in costs originating elsewhere and unions can escalate their wage demands if prices begin to rise. Third, firms can use a strong market position to widen margins in a period of prosperity even if there are no upward pressures on their costs. Fourth, in the nature of the collective bargaining process, key wage bargains in some industries may tend to establish a pattern applied elsewhere. In particular, if the industries with key wage bargains happen to have excess demands and very strong profits, the pattern will tend to pull wages upward more rapidly throughout the economy.

An important, broadly oriented study by the Joint Economic Committee analyzed the workings of these important influences in the 1956–57 inflation. In that period, excess demands that were present in machinery and equipment, automobile, and metals industries led to price increases that were not offset elsewhere. Large wage settlements in these industries with high demand and high profits had pattern-setting effects on many other contracts, thus adding to costs on a broad front.

Rising prices that originate from such a process can affect expectations, jeopardize the stability and balance of an expansion, and create inequities and distortions just as readily as demand inflation. But measures to restrain these price increases by reducing over-all demand will enlarge unemployment and impair the productivity record so important to cost-price stability over the longer run. Policies to improve the operations of markets, increase resource mobility and accelerate technical change can help to increase the economy's resistance to rising prices. But in a world where large firms and large unions play an essential role, the cost-price record will depend heavily upon the responsibility with which they exercise the market power that society entrusts to them.

The need for responsible private action was brought to public attention in the Economic Reports of President Eisenhower's second Administration. Through the major innovation of the guideposts in the Kennedy and Johnson Administrations, this need has since been focused and developed into a national policy to enlist the force of public opinion to maintain cost-price stability. The emergence of such a policy has been all the more important in recent years because of the balance of payments problem that has persisted alongside the domestic need for more expansion.

ECONOMIC POLICY TODAY

Two decades of economic analysis and policy experience have shaped the development of a revised economic policy. By some, current policy has been labeled the "new economics." It draws heavily on the experience and lessons of the past, and it combines both new and old elements. Current policy represents a coordinated and consistent effort to promote balance of over-all supply and aggregate demand — to sustain steady balanced growth at high employment levels with essential price stability.

This approach to policy has several key aspects, not entirely novel by any means. First, it emphasizes a continuous, rather than a cyclical, framework for analyzing economic developments and formulating policies. Stimulus to demand is not confined to avoiding or correcting recession, but rather is applied whenever needed for the promotion of full-utilization and prosperity. Second, in this way, it emphasizes a preventive strategy against the onset of recession. Third, in focusing on balance of the economy, this policy strategy cannot give top priority to balance in the budget. When private investment threatens to outrun saving at full employment, a Government surplus is needed to increase total saving in the economy while restrictive monetary policy may also be called for to restrain investment outlays. When, as in recent years, private saving at full employment tends to outrun actual private investment, the balance should be corrected by budget deficits and expansionary monetary policy. Fourth, it considers the budget and monetary conditions in the framework of a growing economy, recognizing that revenues expand and thereby exert a fiscal drag on demand unless expansionary actions are taken; similarly, it recognizes that money and credit must expand just to keep interest rates from rising. Fifth, this strategy emphasizes the use of a variety of tools to support expansion while simultaneously pursuing other objectives. Manpower policies, selective approaches to control capital outflows, as well as general fiscal and monetary measures, are all part of the arsenal. Sixth, it calls for responsible price-wage actions by labor and management to prevent cost-inflation from impeding the pursuit of full employment. Finally, it makes greater demands on economic forecasting and analysis. The job of the economist is not merely to predict the upturn or the downturn but to judge continuously the prospects for demand in relation to a growing productive capacity.

The Nature of Cyclical Instability

An industrial economy is vulnerable to cumulative upward and downward movements in activity, so evident in our long-term record. While they can have diverse specific causes, these cyclical fluctuations can be explained as the result of imbalances between the rate of growth of productive capacity and the rate of growth of final demands that make use of productive capacity.

During periods of prosperity, a considerable part of the Nation's output is used to increase productive capacity through investment in plant and equipment and business inventories. If demand keeps pace, sales expand and the new capacity turns out to be profitable. Businessmen find that their decisions to increase capacity have been validated and they continue to pursue expansionary investment policies. If, on the other hand, inventory stocks are built up far in advance of need — on the basis of overly optimistic sales forecasts or as an inflation-hedge — businessmen will subsequently wish to cut back their rate of accumulation. Similarly, if outlays for business fixed investment add to productive capacity faster than demand expands, overheads on new capital cut into profits, inducing business firms to trim their capital outlays. Even if businessmen continue to add somewhat to their productive capacity, the mere decline in the rate of expansion can mean an absolute reduction in the demand for capital goods and for output to go into inventories. Payrolls and purchasing power are thereby curtailed and a decline in total demand can result. Thus a slowdown in economic activity is converted into a definite downturn — a recession or depression.

Imbalance can arise because businessmen in the aggregate invest too much and overbuild, creating more capacity than the economy can — even at best — put to productive use. Or alternatively it can stem from "underbuying," a growth of final demand too slow to make use of even moderate additions to capacity. In principle, cyclical movements can also be triggered by overbuilding of new homes and consumer durables.

Overbuilding of inventories — partly encouraged by expectations of rising prices — was probably the key factor in the first postwar downturn, which occurred in 1948. That experience demonstrated that a situation of high total demand could deteriorate rapidly into recession without any change in the basic underlying factors in the private economy or any restraining shift in public policy. In 1953, the sharp decline in defense outlays reduced final demands and precipitated recession; productive capacity became temporarily excessive and investment spending declined. In 1956–57, rapid growth of productive capacity was associated with an investment boom; meanwhile, final demands grew very slowly. It is not possible to deliver a clear verdict on whether more vigorous growth of final demand would have justified the high investment levels then obtaining. But with the slow growth of demand that actually occurred, there was an abrupt decline in plant and equipment spending as well as inventory investment in 1957. In 1959–60, the rate of expansion of capacity (including inventories) was not excessive measured against the capabilities of the economy; the failure of the economy to support that growth of capacity must be attributed to "underbuying," the inadequate expansion of final demand, in an environment of restrictive fiscal and monetary policies.

In the future as in the past, policies to avert recession cannot wait until imbalances develop and the signs of a downturn are clear. The fact that economic activity is rising cannot be an assurance of continued growth if the expansion is too slow to match the growth of productive capacity. Nor can a strong level of investment be relied on to sustain expansion if it threatens an excessive growth of productive capacity. Recognizing these tasks, Government must apply its fiscal and monetary policies continuously to sustain and support a balanced expansion, sometimes by moderating the strength of an excessive investment boom, sometimes by adding to the strength of lagging final demand. The best defense against recession is a policy to sustain continued expansion. In a free economy, fluctuations in private demand will inevitably occur, and the Government will not always have the wisdom or the ability to counteract them. Continued expansion cannot be guaranteed, but recurrent recession need not be accepted as a necessary fact of economic life.

Policy for a Growing Economy

In order to achieve the goal of maximum employment, the Government must coordinate all its policies to take account of the persistent growth of the economy's potential output.

The Problem of Fiscal Drag. One consequence of economic growth is that budgetary policies become more restrictive if they stand still. If tax rates are unchanged, Federal revenues will grow continuously as the economy expands. Meanwhile, if Federal expenditures are held constant in the face of growing revenues, the Federal budget will exert a continuing "fiscal drag" on private demand.

Either increased expenditures or reduced tax rates can offset this influence. A total of these two types of stimulative actions which exactly matched the dollar amount of normal revenue growth would provide a precise offset to fiscal drag (and would leave unchanged the high-employment surplus . . .).

A simple mechanical offset to fiscal drag is not, however, a satisfactory rule for fiscal policy. When aggregate demand threatens to exceed the supply capacity of the economy, some fiscal drag should be allowed to operate. On the other hand, waning strength in private demand points to fiscal action that would more than offset the drag, effecting a desirable decline in the high-employment surplus.

Furthermore, tightness or ease of monetary policy is important in determining appropriate fiscal actions. There is an analog to drag in the monetary area: A growing economy generates rising demands for liquid assets and increasing needs for borrowing. If monetary policies stand still in the sense of holding supplies unchanged, continually tighter credit conditions and higher interest rates will be the result.

Accelerating Growth. The growth of the economy is a major influence on policy; the opposite side of the coin is the major role of policy in influencing potential economic growth. The larger the amount of current output invested in physical and human resources, the more rapidly productivity and the productive capacity of the economy will increase.

A number of policy choices can speed growth by shifting resources into various types of investment. Public investment in human and physical resources can yield rich returns in more rapid economic growth. Some public investments, such as those on research and development, encourage complementary private investment. Outlays for manpower training improve labor skills and productivity. Throughout our history, investment in education has been one of the key contributors to growth. Private investment in plant and equipment is a key determinant of our industrial capacity. It can be stimulated by easing monetary policies. It can also be encouraged by selective tax reductions, such as the investment credit and depreciation reform of 1962 and the reductions in corporate tax rates in 1964 and 1965.

When the economy is below full employment, any stimulative measure is likely to add to private investment, thereby contributing to the growth of potential, as well as to actual, output. But, at full employment, more resources can be devoted to capital formation only if current consumption is restrained. A policy strategy to accelerate growth may therefore point to higher personal income taxes or similar measures to hold consumption below what would otherwise be appropriate.

Choices of Tools. Economic policy has many tools available in pursuing the goals of full employment, rapid growth, price stability, and balance of international payments. The full range of economic objectives must be reflected in the selection of policies to meet particular circumstances.

Policy instruments differ in their impact. Sometimes policy tools can advance the economy toward more than one goal. For example, manpower policies help to maintain price stability at high employment and to promote economic growth. Conflicts may occur, however. For example, high interest rates impinge particularly on investment both at home and abroad, hence somewhat reducing foreign capital outflows but also reducing aggregate demand and slowing economic growth. In the case of potential conflicts, instruments must be used more selectively; for example, moderate changes in interest rates can be supplemented by taxes on foreign investment, like the Interest Equalization Tax.

The potential for timely results differs for various policy instruments. Monetary policy can be altered readily, although its full economic impact will not be immediate. While some restraint or speedup in Federal outlays can be applied by Executive authority alone, tax rate changes must, of course, be approved by the Congress. The speed on congressional action on tax changes has varied. It acted rapidly to increase taxes in 1950, and to reduce excise taxes both in 1954 and

1965. On the other hand, it took 13 months to enact the comprehensive Revenue Act of 1964. Tax revision can help to avoid the necessity for abrupt changes in Federal expenditures, which could require stopping a project before its conclusion or starting a new one with inadequate planning.

Given the possibility for achieving needed short-run stimulus or restraint through changes in taxes, transfer payments, or monetary policy, decisions on expenditures for public services can rest on basic judgments of costs and benefits of public and private spending. The availability of this choice permits resources to be devoted to the highest priority uses.

PREREQUISITES OF SUCCESSFUL POLICY

Choice of the right policy action demands full information about the state of the economy and understanding of its workings. And execution of stabilizing policy requires public understanding and acceptance.

Information

An important requirement of economic policymaking is a firm and timely knowledge of where the economy stands. Spurred by the need for prompt and enlightened decisions, the Federal statistics program has made rapid forward strides in the postwar period, and now provides a much better gauge of current economic developments. Of the 369 monthly series now carried in *Economic Indicators*, the statistical summary prepared by the Council and issued by the Joint Economic Committee, only 60 percent would have been available by the monthly publication date at the time *Economic Indicators* was launched in the late 1940's.

In addition to the information on current developments, a number of anticipatory surveys have been instituted which provide important information on the probable future course of the economy. Outstanding among these is the Commerce-Securities and Exchange Commission survey on plant and equipment; additional important clues to future developments come from the Commerce inventory survey and the Census quarterly survey of consumer buying intentions. Important information also is obtained from private sources including the University of Michigan's Survey Research Center, the National Industrial Conference Board, and McGraw-Hill, Inc.

Yet, our data are not completely satisfactory. The revisions of the national accounts last summer gave evidence of how much we learn later that could have been helpful on a current basis. There are any number of areas — capital stock and capacity, productivity, employee fringe benefits, job vacancies, among them — where there are important gaps and weaknesses in our quantitative information which can be remedied only by expansion of our statistical programs.

Not all the information useful to the Council comes from published sources or takes the form of numbers. The Council, as enjoined by the Act, finds it most useful to consult regularly with business and labor. These consultations provide valuable information and opinions, and also allow the Council to explain and clarify Administration views.

Professional Knowledge

Facts are the essential raw material for analysis, but they require intelligent processing to be useful in guiding policy. The ability of economists to diagnose and forecast on the basis of current facts and to evaluate the impact of alternative policy measures is a key determinant of what policy can do to maintain stable balanced growth.

Our economic knowledge has made great advances in the past generation, but many important questions remain, answers to which should be and can be improved through further research.

There are many quantitative uncertainties in forecasting the strength of private demands. Some of these were illustrated in 1965 when the improvement in profits and sales — coupled with the shifting defense picture — generated a more rapid and greater surge in investment demand than was foreseen initially. Furthermore, the linkage between monetary policy actions and changes in ultimate spending also require more exploration. And even in areas that are more readily quantified, such as the impact on GNP of changes in Government purchases and personal tax reductions, there remains a considerable range of doubt about the timing of the impacts and the specific influences on consumption and investment.

Departing from the domain of aggregative output effects, we need a better understanding of many more specialized problems, such as the functioning of labor markets — how job vacancies are filled, how skill shortages are met, and how excess supplies in one area are ultimately absorbed elsewhere. Such knowledge can be a useful guide to the possibilities for expanding output and employment while avoiding bottlenecks.

But while much remains to be learned about our economy, it would be a disservice to understate the power of economic analysis, and to underrate the substantial contribution of the profession to the successful course of our economy in the postwar period. The Employment Act provided the framework in which this professional contribution could be rendered and be given its proper place in the framing of public policy.

Public Understanding

Not all of the needed improvements in knowledge and understanding are of a technical character. Even though viewed as correct by the professional analyst, policies cannot be applied effectively unless the Congress and the public at large understand how the proposed measures intend to further desirable objectives.

If policy proposals of the Administration are to be converted into legislation, they must be convincing to the Congress. Twenty Annual Economic Reports have explained the rationale for the programs of four Presidents. And the Joint Economic Committee has rendered invaluable service in contributing to an understanding of general economic policy and specific proposals. The principles of fiscal policy and their implications for tax and expenditure legislation have been central to the Nation's economic education in the past 20 years. The great increase in understanding is best seen in the sophisticated current level of public discussion.

Proper understanding of policies by the public, moreover, contributes to the very success of the policy measures. In the absence of public understanding, there can be perverse reactions. If people read policies to maintain price stability as an announcement that inflation has arrived, rather than an exercise of determination to avoid it, destabilized prices may be the result. If people see steps to combat recession as a sign of panic rather than a support to the economy, this too can have adverse psychological effects. In particular, a firm appreciation by the American people of the rationale of wage-price guideposts is essential to make them effective and to limit the need for active participation by Government. It is the public that gets hurt by irresponsible wage-price decisions, and public reaction can be the best reminder to those with market power of their social responsibility.

BELA BALASSA

Whither French Planning*

French planning has been perhaps the most widely publicized of all European planning. Professor Balassa thoroughly dissects French planning and raises fundamental questions about the adjustment of planning to an open economy. He shows how this issue has been increasingly forced upon the planners as the world economy has become increasingly liberalized in the postwar period and how planning techniques must change in response to these altered circumstances.

I

THIS PAPER CONSIDERS the ways in which medium-term planning will be affected by "opening" the French economy through the dismantling of protective barriers and entry into the Common Market.[1] The proposition is advanced that, in a system of fixed exchange rates, the opening of a national economy provides new constraints for the planning process and necessitates the transformation of the system of economic planning.

In an open economy, increases in the prices of traded goods are subject to a "micro" and a "macro" constraint. On the one hand, entrepreneurs have to limit price increases in order to avoid the loss of foreign markets or the encroachment of foreign firms on domestic markets; on the other, governments cannot accept a continuing balance-of-payments deficit to which the inflationary process gives rise. At the same time, foreign competition increases uncertainty in the decision-making process and reduces the reliability of forecasts.

These constraints are hardly operative in a closed economy, however. Foreign competition provides little restraint to increases in

[1] The expression "medium-term planning" (*planification à moyen terme*) is used to refer to the practice of preparing four- and five-year plans for the French economy.

* Reprinted by permission of the publishers from Bela Balassa, *The Quarterly Journal of Economics*, pp. 537–555, Cambridge, Mass.: Harvard University Press, Copyright, 1965, by the President and Fellows of Harvard College.

prices in this case, and governments can utilize various direct measures to correct a balance-of-payments deficit. In turn, the sheltering of the economy from foreign influences reduces uncertainties relating to production and investment decisions, and the absence of external constraints allows for the separation of medium-term planning and short-term policy-making.

II

In attempting to evaluate the "openness" of national economies, we may first consider the share of foreign buyers and sellers in the domestic production and consumption of traded goods.[2] A high proportion of exports to domestic production gives expression to the relative importance of foreign markets for home producers, while a high ratio of imports to domestic expenditure provides an indication of the extent of competition between domestic and foreign enterprises in the home market.

To make appropriate comparisons, it would be necessary to utilize input-output tables that provide information on the allocation of imports between intermediate and final uses, and on the utilization of services as inputs in producing traded goods. Input-output tables are not available for the entire period under consideration, however, and we have chosen to relate the value of exports and imports[3] to value added in the production of traded goods instead. Further, in order to abstract from the impact of changing competitiveness on exports and imports, and the effects of nontrade items on their ratio, we have used the average of the two figures to indicate the relative degree of openness of national economies.[4]

If we take the year 1953 as representative of the period preceding the Common Market's establishment, we find that the French economy had a closed character as compared with other European economies of similar size and, *a fortiori*, in comparison with smaller countries, such as Belgium and the Netherlands. In that year, the average ratio of exports and imports to value added in the sectors producing traded goods was 17.3 per cent in France, as against 20.1

[2] Agricultural, mineral and manufactured products.

[3] Imports have been expressed in c.i.f. prices since, under the assumption that the prices of imports and marginal costs in the domestic production of import-competing goods are equalized, these provide the relevant comparison.

[4] This measure was used also in Jean Bénard, "Le Marché Commun Europeen et l'avenir de la planification francaise," *Revue Economique*, XV (Sept. 1964), 756–84.

per cent in Italy, 22.0 in Germany, 45.6 in the United Kingdom, 70.4 in Belgium, and 91.0 per cent in the Netherlands. But, in the case of France, it would be incorrect to consider total exports and imports, since the overseas territories were in fact part of the French market-area, and the objective of balance-of-payments equilibrium related to the entire franc area rather than to metropolitan France. Excluding trade with these territories, the above ratio is calculated as 10.8 per cent for France in 1953 — substantially lower than the results shown for other countries. And if only exports are considered, the French economy seems to have been less open than that of the United States.[5]

Merchandise exports and imports include agricultural products, the domestic markets of which are sheltered in most industrial countries, as well as raw materials the imports of which are complementary rather than competitive with domestic production. Greater interest attaches, therefore, to the relative importance of foreign trade in the case of manufactured goods. At the same time, data on production and trade are available for the main categories of manufactured goods in France, so that we can avoid the difficulties associated with the comparison of the value of trade and value added in production.

In 1953 France sent to foreign countries, on the average, 11 per cent of her manufacturing production and derived 12.6 per cent of her consumption of manufactured goods from imports. The share of exports (imports) in domestic production (consumption) was the highest in the textile and clothing industries, followed by chemicals, while the relevant ratios did not reach 10 per cent in the case of machinery and transportation equipment, lumber and paper, and construction materials.

These comparisons give some indication of the relative degree of openness of the French economy, but they have to be supplemented by information regarding the instruments utilized for regulating exports and imports. The instruments in question include tariffs, taxes, subsidies, quantitative restrictions, and devaluation. The French economy of the 1950's provides an example for the employment of all of these measures. It appears that, prior to the establishment of the Common Market, the combined use of taxes, tariffs, and quotas led to the virtual exclusion of imports competing with domestic production in France, while subsidies helped French producers to export in cases when they were not competitive. Still,

---

[5] The relevant ratios are 9.0 and 10.6 per cent, respectively.

only one-half of the sales of manufactured goods outside metropolitan France went to foreign countries in 1953 while the remainder found safe markets in the associated territories.

The closed character of her economy made it possible for France to maintain a high rate of economic growth in an inflationary environment.[6] The various policy instruments used by the government simultaneously ensured home markets for domestic producers and equilibrium in the balance of payments. With the OEEC liberalization measures — only partially applied in France until 1958 — and with entry into the Common Market, the situation changed, however. The French economy increasingly assumed an open character, and the government had to forego the use of a number of policy instruments employed in earlier periods. To prepare the French economy for this new situation, and to improve the competitive position of French producers while attaining external equilibrium, the devaluation of the franc became necessary. Devaluation was undertaken on two occasions in rapid succession in 1957 and 1958, and the external value of the franc was reduced by nearly 30 per cent.

The opening of the French economy finds expression in the figures relating to the share of foreign trade in production and in consumption. While exports to foreign countries accounted for 9.0 per cent of value added in the production of traded goods in 1953, this ratio surpassed 15 per cent in 1960, and reached 17.5 per cent in 1963; in the latter year, the corresponding ratio for imports was 19.2 per cent as compared with 12.7 per cent in 1953. At the same time, the markets of the former associated territories have gradually been opened to foreign competition. Were we to consider these as foreign markets, the average ratio of exports and imports to value added in the production of traded goods would amount to 22.1 per cent in 1963.

Similar results are shown in regard to manufactured goods. The proportion of exports to production approximately doubled between 1953 and 1963, with larger than average increases observed in the case of machinery and transportation equipment. The share of imports in domestic production increased in a parallel fashion in individual industries, the exception being textiles and clothing where a slight decline is shown.

These developments have necessitated changes in the system of economic planning. The planning of foreign trade has assumed increasing importance and the dichotomy of medium-term planning

---

[6] In the period 1950–57, a growth rate of GNP of 4.8 per cent put France at sixth place among industrial countries, while France led the field in price increases with the GNP deflator rising at an average annual rate of 6.2 per cent.

and short-term policy-making has given place to an attempt to coordinate the two. Correspondingly, there has been a shift in emphasis from physical to financial balances in the preparation of the plan.

III

The foreign trade sector played little role in the preparation of the first two Plans for Modernization and Equipment. Export prospects and import requirements did not receive detailed consideration, and while balance-of-payments equilibrium was listed among the objectives of the Second Plan, this was to be attained by keeping imports at the 1952 level in 1957, the terminal year of the Plan. At the same time, the continuation of the system of subsidies was foreseen in order to obtain balance-of-payments equilibrium through an expansion of exports.[7] . . .

But quantitative restrictions were by-and-large abolished in the years following, and entry into the European Common Market brought about a reduction of duties not only on imports from the partner countries, but also on imports from the outside. Correspondingly, instead of stagnation, imports from foreign countries rose by 25.2 per cent between 1956 and 1961 while, with the help of the two devaluations, exports increased by 71.0 per cent instead of the planned figure of 33.5 per cent.[8]

With the opening of the French economy, the foreign trade sector has assumed increasing importance in the Plan, and efforts have been made to improve upon the methods of projecting international trade. In the course of the preparation of the Fourth Plan (1962–65), export-projections were made (a) for large commodity groups, assuming a continuation of past trends in export/GNP ratios, and (b) on a geographical basis, by extrapolating past relationships, with a subsequent confrontation of the results obtained by the use of the two methods. Imports were also projected for groups of products, when the continuation of past relationships between imports and GNP was generally assumed. These estimates were subsequently adjusted by taking account of the findings of the Industrial Commissions. Finally, a more detailed commodity breakdown is used in making estimates for the Fifth Plan (1966–70), and it is also attempted to project French exports and imports in the framework of EEC trade.

Despite the improvements in methods of projecting foreign trade,

[7] *Deuxième Plan de Modernisation et d'Equipment* (1954–1957), N°. 56–342 de 27 mars 1956, *Journal Officiel*, No. 1057, 1956, pp. 151–53.

[8] J. Bénard, C. Roux, and C. Girardeau, *op. cit.*, p. 120.

the problem remains that the opening of the economy has introduced a considerable degree of uncertainty in planning and has reduced the freedom of action of the policy-maker. Uncertainty is related to production and consumption decisions made abroad, which are considered only in their reflection on foreign trade, and to changes in international price-relationships. While in the preparation of the plan it is assumed that prices will move in a parallel fashion in France and abroad, trade is affected by disparate changes in the general price level in individual national economies, as well as by changes in relative prices within each country.

Uncertainties relating to the estimation of trade flows will increase in importance as the process of "opening" of the French economy continues. In fact, according to preliminary version of the Fifth Plan, during the period 1965–70 annual increases of 9.4 per cent in imports would accompany a 5 per cent rate of growth of the gross domestic product.[9] The implications of these uncertainties for planning procedures will next be considered.

IV

In preparing the first four Plans, the French planners utilized a system of "physical" balances to compare resources and requirements for individual industries and to establish consistency among the plans of these industries. The two Plans for Modernization and Equipment (1949–53 and 1954–57) dealt principally with some large sectors, without attempting to ensure consistency on the national economy level. But, beginning with the Third Plan, an input-output table was used to provide a general framework for planning and to eliminate inconsistencies in the forecasts for individual industries.

The physical balances, then, provided guidelines for the entrepreneurs, inasmuch as they received information concerning the demand for their products on the part of final and intermediate users. With a small, and well regulated, foreign sector, projections could be made with a reasonable degree of confidence for a chosen rate of growth of national income, and could serve as a basis for investment decisions. At the same time, the government could take action by using the various fiscal instruments at its disposal, as well as its credit granting powers, to ensure the fulfillment of the plan.

[9] Commissariat Général du Plan d'Equipment et de la Productivité, *Rapport sur les Principales Options du Ve Plan* — Projet de loi portant approbation d'un rapport sur les principales options qui commande la préparation du Ve Plan, Assemblée Nationale, N°. 1154, Nov. 5, 1964, Vol. III, p. 4.

Uncertainties for business decision-making have increased, how-ever, as the foreign sector has assumed importance and the possibilities for sheltering domestic industry from foreign competition have been greatly reduced. The consequences of the opening of the French market to foreign competition were observable already in the course of the execution of the Third Plan, when in several industries (e.g., automobiles, refrigerators) the unplanned rise of imports and the nonfulfillment of export targets were largely responsible for production falling short of expectations. Uncertainties are magnified in regard to investment decisions since marginal changes in production may lead to a doubling or scrapping of an investment program.

Under these circumstances, the government can hardly take responsibility for the correctness of the final and intermediate demand forecasts communicated to individual industries, and there is a tendency to make credit and fiscal policy more neutral in their effects on various branches of industry. At any rate, in conjunction with the liberalization of trade and participation in the EEC, France had to forego the use of a number of instruments that could be utilized before. To cite an official report: "No special measure is available anymore that would permit the regulation of imports, there is no mechanism that would guarantee that export objectives could be regarded with confidence. Everything depends on international competition."[10]

More specifically, the acceptance of obligations in the OECD and participation in the Common Market means that various fiscal instruments that were used to favor home production over imports, and one domestic industry over another, cannot further be employed. These include subsidies, tax-incentives, interest allowances, quantitative restrictions, and tariffs on intra-EEC trade. Moreover, with monetary integration, devaluation ceases to be an instrument of national economy policy, while international capital movements and the right of establishment by enterprises of member countries within the EEC make it difficult to pursue a selective credit policy.

At the same time, entrepreneurs increasingly orient their activity in a Common Market rather than in a national framework. Not only do they take account of foreign competition in their production and investment decisions, but there also appears to be a tendency to specialize in narrower ranges of product. Specialization, in turn, may take place as a result of market pressures or may be subject to formal

[10] Commissariat Général du Plan et Services des Etudes Economiques et Financières, "Projet de Rapport du Groupe d'Equilibre de la Commission de l'Economie Général du Financement du Plan," June 1961 (mimeo.) p. 57.

or informal agreements among firms located in the member countries.

Mention should further be made of the observed tendency to subdivide the production process in the Common Market countries without regard to national frontiers. This can take place in the framework of large international firms, such as Phillips and Siemens, or through the importation of parts, components, and accessories. Increased reliance on intermediate products of foreign origin also necessitates changes in planning procedures as firms tend to make their choice between domestic and foreign suppliers on the basis of price rather than accepting government arbitration.[11]

In conjunction with these developments, industrialists wish to increase their freedom of action, as indicated by the declaration of the organization of French employers, adopted in January, 1965. The declaration asserts that "in matters of the management of business, the authority [for making decisions] cannot be divided" and concludes that "above all, the illusions of a systematic *dirigisme,* whose failure can be now ascertained everywhere, should be renounced."[12] While there appears to be a considerable degree of dissension in *Patronat* circles regarding these conclusions, the document is representative of changes in management thinking that have taken place since the establishment of the Common Market.

These considerations point towards a de-emphasis on physical balances. In fact, a considerable degree of flexibility has been introduced in the Fifth Plan and the detailed production forecasts are no longer regarded as targets. Instead, more emphasis is given to structural objectives that relate to concentration and rationalization in individual industries.[13] At the same time, financial balances have assumed increased importance in the plan.

Financial balances are designed to indicate the conditions of reaching financial equilibrium with the attendant distribution of incomes, their allocation between consumption and saving, and the modalities of financing investment activity — the ways and means of transforming savings into productive investment. Thus, in the financial

---

[11] It has been reported that in case of differences of opinion in the cotton yarn and garment industry "it is actually arbitration by the supreme agencies of the Plan that will establish cotton yarn imports within the framework of the Plan forecasts, both for the industry that weaves these yarns and for the ready-to-wear garment industry that uses them." CEPES, *French and Other National Economic Plans for Growth* (New York: Committee for Economic Development, 1963), p. 68.

[12] Declaration du Conseil national du patronat francais, Jan. 19, 1965.

[13] Cf. e.g., *The Economist,* May 23, 1964, p. 852.

balances estimates are given of the sources and the utilization of incomes of the economic agents, with a view to arriving at an income distribution that is noninflationary and, at the same time, provides adequate investment funds. The framework of financial balances is also used to ascertain in what form financing for new investments will be available *and* acceptable to the entrepreneur.

Before the preparation of the Fifth Plan, financial balances were little more than a formality. The balances were prepared in constant prices so that no account could be taken of the rising trend in the relative prices of services. At the same time, it was assumed that wages would rise *pari passu* with productivity, and gross profits would increase at the same rate as wages. Still, work done under the Fourth Plan provided the basis for the subsequent analysis of the *circuits de financement* of new investments.

Financial balances have assumed importance in the course of the preparation of the Fifth Plan, however. The explanation is easy to find. While at the time when the French economy was reasonably free of foreign influences, the plan could be carried out in an inflationary environment and medium-term planning was independent of short-term policy-making, price stability has become a principal objective of the Plan under present conditions. Medium-term planning has now little value without a policy of stability since the deterioration of the balance of payments and the fiasco of investment plans following a decline in competitiveness would make the Plan inoperative.

Financial balances thus give expression to objectives for medium-term planning as well as for short-term policy-making, when the coordination of the two is further served by the use of *clignotants* that would give danger signals in case stability is threatened. But financial balances only provide a framework for policy-making, and their practical usefulness will depend on the availability of instruments to ensure the fulfillment of the appropriate objectives. Before turning to this question, however, it will be useful to review the recent experience of the French economy regarding prices, foreign trade, and the financing of investments.

V

The devaluations of 1957 and 1958 gave the French economy a competitive advantage over most other industrial countries; in addition to correcting for the disparate changes in prices experienced during the previous period, they also made the French franc an undervalued currency. Correspondingly, in trade with countries outside of the franc area, the deficit of about 3 billion francs in 1957 gave place to an export surplus of similar magnitude in 1961.[14] Inflationary developments have since worked to the disadvantage of France, however, and within two years her merchandise trade surplus by and large disappeared.

The GNP deflator indicates a 24.3 per cent rise in the general price level in France between 1958 and 1963. Among other major industrial countries, Italy experienced the largest increase with 19.7 per cent, and the United States the smallest, 5.2 per cent. For the same period, the implicit price index of manufactured goods derived from national income statistics shows a 19.3 per cent rise in France, while price increases did not exceed 10 per cent elsewhere.[15]

Price increases immediately following a devaluation can be explained by the effects of higher import prices on the domestic price level. But the inflationary process continued in subsequent years, and showed signs of acceleration after 1960. Increases were the largest in service prices, hence the observed differences between the GNP deflator and consumer prices on the one hand, and prices of manufactured goods on the other. . . . In the latter case, international competition appears to have restrained price increases.[16] Correspondingly, profit margins and the rate of self-financing declined. . . .

Inflationary pressures thus had a double effect in France: the rise in the prices of manufactured goods led to a deterioration of the French balance-of-payments position, yet price increases were not sufficient to maintain profit-margins and the rate of self-financing. In fact, the rate of self-financing in private enterprises (the ratio of business savings to gross investment) declined from 75 per cent in 1960 to 65 per cent in 1962, and to 62 per cent in 1963. These results are explained by increases in wage costs; in the face of a tight labor market, wages increased at an annual rate of over 8 per cent and, in the first two years of the Fourth Plan, the disposable incomes of households rose at a rate of double that of the volume of production.[17]

In conjunction with these developments, the rate of increase of productive investments fell behind the planned targets (5.9 instead

[14] Merchandise trade, imports adjusted to an f.o.b. basis.

[15] OECD, *Statistics of National Accounts, 1950–1961,* and *Supplements.*

[16] The years 1959 and 1960 provide an exception. At that time, the price advantage due to the two devaluations still permitted producers of manufactured goods to raise their prices at the same rate as that shown for other sectors.

[17] *Rapport sur les Principales Options du Vᵉ Plan,* II, 35.

of 6.4 per cent on an annual basis with much of the increase taking place in the first year of the Plan), while the rise in private consumption exceeded expectations by a considerable margin (6.6 instead of 5.2 per cent). The high rate of growth of private consumption and price increases in the manufacturing sector were accompanied by a deterioration in the trade balance: imports rose at an annual rate of 14.1 per cent instead of the planned rate of 5.3 per cent while exports increased by 3.5 per cent instead of the projected rate of 4.7 per cent.[18]

These adverse changes have necessitated the application of a policy of stabilization, officially announced in September 1963. This entailed the use of various monetary and fiscal instruments, such as credit restraint, balancing the government budget, and a price freeze; at the same time, it was expected that the general deflationary measures and resistance to the wage claims of public employees would be followed by a slowing down of wage increases in the private sector.

The stabilization policy has in fact led to a decline in the rate of increase of prices: the consumer price index rose by 2.1 per cent between the third quarter of 1963 and 1964, as compared with an increase of 5.3 per cent between the corresponding periods in 1962 and 1963, and 5.8 per cent the year before. The effects on wages were slower in coming. Hourly wage rates in manufacturing rose by 7.4 per cent in the above period, as against increases of 8.6 and 9.2 per cent in the preceding years, entailing an acceleration in the rise of real wages.[19] In the third quarter of the year 1964, however, when the deflationary measures succeeded in easing the situation on the labor market, the rise of nominal and real wages was at a long-time low: 1.2 and 0.3 per cent, respectively.[20]

But profit margins have hardly been helped by the stabilization policy. Although the upward movement of wages decelerated, this has not been sufficient to counterbalance the effects of the price freeze. The continuation of the squeeze on profit margins, and the stagnation in manufacturing production experienced during 1964, have been accompanied by a slowing down in investment activity; private industrial investments fell somewhat in 1964 and a further decline is projected for the year 1965.[21]

[18] Institut National de la Statistique et des Etudes Economiques, *Rapport sur les Comptes de la Nation de l'année 1963* (Paris, 1964), p. 13.

[19] OECD, *General Statistics,* Nov. 1964.

[20] *Le Monde,* Nov. 27, 1964.

[21] INSEE, *Etudes et Conjoncture,* various issues.

The adverse effects of the stabilization program on production and investment, along with its apparent success in reducing the rate of increase of prices and wages, point to the need for choosing between the continuation of "stop and go" measures and application of a policy of expansion *cum* stability. The French policymakers appear to have opted for the second alternative and this choice has found expression in the document on the general orientation of the Fifth Plan, submitted to, and accepted by, the Assemblée Nationale.

VI

Under conditions of an open economy, the planners face the double problem of maintaining price stability and ensuring the financing of private investments. In view of our previous discussion, price stability is necessary both for expanding production and for equilibrating the balance of payments. At the same time, the competitive position of French industry could hardly be maintained without an adequate rate of investment that would permit the rise of productivity foreseen in the Plan.

As regards the financing of private investments, the accent is put on self-financing in the Fifth Plan, and a return to a rate of self-financing of 70 per cent is proposed.[22] Various explanations are given to justify this choice. To begin with, reference is made to the reluctance of entrepreneurs to augment their indebtedness, and the increasing cost of indebtedness due to the restraining effect of foreign competition on the prices of manufactured goods.[23] It is further argued that competition in the Common Market, as well as in the world economy, requires the concentration of production in larger enterprises, while the French financial market is too weak to supply adequate financing.[24]

One may add that since the propensity to save is substantially higher for profit receivers than for wage earners, an increase in profits would contribute more to investment than an equivalent rise in wages. Correspondingly, an acceleration in the rate of investment activity would require an increase in the share of profits at the expense of

[22] This figure relates to nonagricultural public and private enterprises taken together, for which the relevant ratio was nearly 80 per cent during the 1950's, 70 per cent in 1960 and 64 per cent in 1963 with a further decline foreseen in 1964 and 1965 (*Rapport sur les Principales Options du Ve Plan*, II, 32, 58).

[23] With the rapid rate of inflation, the interest cost of borrowing was practically nil during much of the fifties.

[24] *Ibid.*, p. 32. See also the report of Robert Pelletier to the Conseil Economique et Social (Dec. 1964).

wages. This is indeed an apparent objective of the Fifth Plan, as indicated by the projections contained in its preliminary version: a 4.9 per cent annual increase of wages and salaries is foreseen for the period 1965–70, while the double requirements of increasing productive investments at an annual rate of 5.7 per cent and raising the rate of self-financing to 70 per cent[25] would entail a rise of profits by about 9 per cent a year.

The attainment of the twin objectives of price stability and increasing self-financing of investments would, then, necessitate a slowing down in the rise of wages and salaries; on a per capita basis, the relevant estimates are 5.1 per cent a year for 1960–65 and 3.3 per cent for 1965–70.[26] There are three ways of keeping down the rate of increase of wages: the application of an incomes policy, voluntary restraint, and the "easing" of conditions in the labor market.

A voluminous literature exists on the problems and possibilities of an incomes policy,[27] and several attempts have been made to put such a policy into practice. Well known is the experience of the Netherlands, widely quoted as an example of the success of an incomes policy until 1963, when it broke down in the face of the increasing tightness of the Dutch labor market.

This is not to say that an incomes policy could not be successful, if the conditions for its success were fulfilled. These conditions include an understanding between the government, the employers, and the trade unions on national economic objectives, in general, and on the need to limit wage increases, in particular. Such an understanding appears to be in the making in the United Kingdom under the Labor government, as indicated by the "treaty on incomes" accepted by the three parties in December, 1964. It also has possibilities in Scandinavia where the dependence on exports contributed to voluntary restraint in the past. The situation in France appears to be different, however.

To begin with, the largest trade union in France, the Confédération Générale du Travail, is communist-dominated and it would hardly agree with the government on a policy of wage restraint — or, for that matter, on national economic objectives. But the other trade unions, the C.F.T.C. and the Force Ouvrière, do not appear to be inclined to accept such a policy either, partly because of their fear

[25] *Rapport sur les Principales Options du Ve Plan*, III, 4, 11.

[26] *Ibid.*, III, 11.

[27] Cf., e.g., the publications of the OECD: William Fellner *et al.*, *The Problem of Rising Prices* (Paris, 1961), *Policies for Price Stability* (Paris, 1963), and *Policies for Prices, Profits and Other Non-wage Incomes* (Paris, 1964).

of losing members to the C.G.T. and partly because they apparently believe that private enterprise would be the sole beneficiary.

In this connection, note should be taken of recent discussions on the self-financing of private enterprise in France. Since the Club Jean-Moulin, an influential private organization, has characterized self-financing as an "indirect tax levied on the public," several commentators have raised the question as to whether wage earners would be willing to accept the sacrifice involved in increased self-financing if the benefits of the latter accrued solely to entrepreneurs and shareholders.[28] While this argument takes no account of the indirect benefits of increasing investment activity for wage earners in the form of higher productivity and real wages, it is symptomatic of the position taken by a large part of the French public. It has also found its way into a speech made by the former Gaullist Prime Minister, Michel Debré, during the parliamentary debate on the general orientations of the Fifth Plan, when Debré declared that "it would be good if the workers participated in the enrichment self-financing entails."[29]

Trade unions are not only opposed to increasing the share of profits in national income associated with a rise in the rate of self-financing; they also wish to change the existing distribution of incomes in favor of the wage earners. This demand has been expressed in the counterplan prepared by the small leftist Parti Socialiste Unifié as well as by union officials.[30]

In a more general context, one may argue that the attenuation of social conflicts, experienced in the United States and in Continental Europe north of the Rhine, has been of more limited scope in France. At the same time, the opposing interests of social classes hinder the application of a national policy, when the situation is not helped by the fact that many regard the present regime as the government of the Right.[31]

It may further be added that the difficulties of restraining wage

28 *Le Monde,* Oct. 4–5, 1964, Nov. 25, 29–30, 1964.

29 *Le Monde,* Nov. 27, 1964.

30 Cf. "Le Contre-Plan présénte par le P.S.U." and statements by the C.G.T., C.F.T.C. and F.O. made on the occasion of the parliamentary discussion of the options of the Fifth Plan. Also, *Le Monde,* Nov. 25, 1964.

31 For a socialist view on the lack of understanding between the government and the wage earners, see the article of André Philip, in the Oct. 4–5, 1964, issue of *Le Monde,* and Defferre's speech during the parliamentary debate on the general orientations of the Fifth Plan, reported in the Nov. 27, 1964 issue of *Le Monde.* See also the conclusion of an article of the leftist *Express,* dealing with the chances of an incomes policy in France: "A conservative government evokes the distrust of the wage earners who, in turn, embarrass it through social conflicts" (*Express,* Dec. 19–20, 1964).

increases are compounded by reason of the fact that their previous experience with rising living costs makes workers reluctant to accept smaller increases in nominal wages than in the past. Finally, there is little evidence that the opening of the French economy would have led unions to promote voluntary wage restraint so as to avoid cutbacks in production and employment due to foreign competition.

These considerations point to the conclusion that, under present-day conditions, the chances for a successful incomes policy in France are rather slim. The obstacles in the way of such a policy are also indicated by the fact that the Conseil Économique and Social has failed to approve the report prepared by Pierre Massé, the Commissaire Général du Plan, on "the principles and criteria" of an incomes policy.[32] Thus, not only is there no general agreement on such a policy, but neither has the position of the government on the means and objectives of an incomes policy been clarified.

Failing an incomes policy and voluntary restraint, actions taken for easing the pressures on the labor market can provide an alternative. A negative relationship between the rate of unemployment and the rate of increase of wages has been shown in the case of the United Kingdom, the United States, and Canada, and this relationship — Phillips' Law — appears to apply to Continental countries also.[33] Correspondingly, a restraint on aggregate demand would reduce the observed tendency for wage increases.

This solution appears to have been chosen in carrying out the policy of stabilization in France. The result has been an increase in unemployment and a decline in vacancies, while working hours have been reduced for a substantial segment of the labor force. The easing of the labor market has weakened the bargaining position of the wage earners, resulting in a decline in the rate of increase of hourly wages: 1.2 per cent in the third quarter of 1964, as compared with 2.3 per cent in the same period of 1962 and 1.8 per cent in 1963.[34]

The preliminary version of the Fifth Plan also provides indica-

[32] *Rapport sur la politique des Revenus établi à la suite de la Conférence des Revenus* (Oct. 1963–Jan. 1964), Paris, La Documentation Francaise, 1964.

[33] Cf. A. W. Phillips, "The Relation between Unemployment and the Rate of Change of Money Wage Rates in the United Kingdom, 1862–1957," *Economica,* XXV (Nov. 1958), 283–99; G. L. Perry, "The Determinants of Wage Rate Changes and the Inflation-Unemployment Trade-off for the United States," *The Review of Economic Studies,* XXXI (Oct. 1964), 287–308; S. F. Kaliski, "The Relation between Unemployment and the Rate of Change of Money Wages in Canada," *International Economic Review,* Vol. 5 (Jan. 1964), pp. 1–33; and B. Balassa, "Some Observations on Mr. Beckerman's Export-Propelled Growth Model: A Rejoinder," *Economic Journal,* LXXIV (Mar. 1964), 240–42.

[34] *Le Monde,* Nov. 27, 1964.

tions of the government's intention to obtain the objectives of price stability and increased self-financing through a *détente* on the labor market. The reduction of the target rate of growth of GNP from the original 5.5 to 5.0 per cent points in this direction, for example. It is a different question whether the, quite respectable, 5 per cent growth rate would be compatible with the requirements of stability. The answer to this question depends, among other things, on developments in other countries. . . .

The attainment of the objectives of price stability and increasing self-financing would, then, necessitate a slowing down in the rise of wages and salaries. Given the existing political and social conflicts in France, it can hardly be expected that these goals will be attained through voluntary wage restraint or an incomes policy. Correspondingly, the logic of planning in an open economy appears to have led the French toward a "liberal" solution — one that uses deflationary measures in the short run and sacrifices the objective of a higher growth rate in the long run for the sake of stability, and creates a *détente* on the labor market in order to restrain wage increases.

PART THREE

SOVIET-AREA PLANNING

ALEX NOVE

Soviet Economic Progress*

Against a background of rapid change and great controversy, Professor Nove ably highlights current planning problems in the Soviet Union. As his article indicates, there is visible tension between the need for change to bring about more efficient economic performance and the difficulty in terms of the organic disturbances of Soviet society which change would entail. He shows how reform in the past has foundered and tended to have a cyclical character. It is always extremely difficult, in any society, to reconcile all the different interests affected by large-scale change.

NEARLY TEN YEARS have passed since I attempted an analysis of Soviet economic growth in an article in this *Review*.[1] At that time it was proper to challenge the general scepticism, to point to the realities of Soviet industrial achievement, and to see what would happen if the

---

[1] "The Pace of Soviet Economic Development," in the April, 1956, issue of this *Review*.

* From A. Nove, "Soviet Economic Progress," *Lloyd's Bank Review* (October, 1965), pp. 15–33. Reprinted by permission of the author and *Lloyd's Bank Review*. Professor Nove wrote this essay early in 1965.

then existing growth-rates were extrapolated into the future. Since then, opinion has swung from one extreme to another.

The sputnik, in 1957, provided spectacular proof of Soviet scientific progress and gave the lie to those who imagined that all Soviet claims were founded merely on propaganda. This led some observers to the view that all Soviet claims were, on the whole, true, and so to exaggerated and indeed alarmist conclusions about the U.S.S.R.'s ultimate triumph in the "peaceful co-existence" competition. Khrushchev, indeed, shared such views, and historians will probably regard 1957–58 as the high-point of Soviet economic-political optimism. Growth was rapid, the West was visibly impressed, under-developed countries were glad to receive Soviet aid, whose political impact was such as to hearten Khrushchev and to depress Western analysts.

Gradually, however, the picture became less favourable. Growth-rates began to decline in industry, and they virtually ceased in agriculture even before the disastrous harvest of 1963. The impact of Soviet aid diminished, even though its volume increased. The effect of the quarrel with China, and of the evident weakening of Soviet leadership of world communism, had adverse effects both internally and externally. After 1958, moreover, a slow-down in growth was accompanied by increasing evidence of a fundamental crisis of the entire system of planning. Reacting to difficulties and shortfalls as they arose, Khrushchev gradually lost both his confidence and his *bonhomie,* interfered increasingly with economic decision-making, launched a series of confusing reorganizations, offended many powerful interests. His exit from the political scene in October, 1964, was not, of course, due solely to considerations of economic policy. However, most of his apparently purely political difficulties can be traced to his efforts to cope with economic problems.

As these difficulties mounted, Western commentators changed their tone. In some instances this was a reaction to the overestimation of the "Soviet economic menace," so prevalent in 1958. It produced works with such titles as *They are not ten feet tall.* (Agreed: they are not.) Other analysts very properly drew attention to, and analysed the causes of, the clear and evident slow-down in Soviet growth, though the extent of the slow-down has been the subject of some controversy. There is perhaps a danger that, once again, we may underestimate Soviet economic power. It seems a fitting moment, therefore, to review the facts and to make some estimate of where matters now stand.

GROWTH SLOWS DOWN

First of all, there is no doubt that Soviet growth has shown a tendency to slow down. This can be shown clearly enough using Soviet official statistics. True, the validity of Soviet output indexes has been very legitimately questioned, but there is no particular reason for supposing that the degree of their unreliability has altered in the course of recent years. So the deceleration which they show seems genuine, even though the actual percentages may be taken with a pinch of salt.

TABLE I

(per cent increase over previous year)

	National income[1]	Gross industrial production	Gross agricultural production
	%	%	%
1954	12	13	5
1955	12	12	11
1956	11	11	13.5
1957	7	10	2
1958	12	10	10.5
1959	8	11	0.5
1960	8	10	2.5
1961	7	9	2.5
1962	6	9.5	1.5
1963	4	8	−7
1964	7	7	12

[1] Soviet definition, i.e. material goods only; it includes construction, and also transport of trade in goods.

As might be expected, year-by-year fluctuations in agricultural output, due to weather, affect the growth in national income: thus the relatively high 1964 figure is due to the big increase in the harvest, following the disastrous year 1963. However, the downward trend is unmistakable. It becomes even more so if one looks at Soviet claims for earlier years. Thus, the war-affected years excepted, the increases in industrial output in 1963 and 1964 represent the lowest officially reported growth-rates for any years since 1933; while the average rate of growth of national income in the three years 1962–64 is the lowest three-year average since the end of the civil war.

This, be it repeated, is the picture taking the official statistics. It is highly probable that, since 1950, these have become less prone to exaggeration than they were before. All the same, the fact of deceleration is there. Soviet economists are well aware of it, and this awareness has stimulated the search for remedies, for greater efficiency, a more rational utilization of investment resources and so on.

DECLINE IN INVESTMENT RATE

The causes of the slow-down are many, and have tended to reinforce one another. Some Soviet writers have been alarmed by a fall in the "effectiveness of capital": the increment of output from a given volume of investment has declined. So far as this has occurred, it is due mainly to the poor performance of agriculture, of which much more will be said later. However, a more obvious immediate cause of the fall in growth-rates has been a marked slow-down in the rise in the volume of investment. The following table leaves one in no doubt of this.

TABLE 2 — TOTAL INVESTMENTS, INCLUDING COLLECTIVE-FARM AND PRIVATE

(per cent increase over previous year)

	%
1957	12.7
1958	16.3
1959	13.3
1960	7.9
1961	4.4
1962	4.7
1963	5.2

A fall such as this in the rate of growth of investment would of itself be expected to lead to a deceleration of growth. The question immediately arises: Why did such a fall occur? Partly it reflects, and is a reflection of, a slow-down in the growth of the output of investment goods and also of the volume of building work done. But this is simply another way of saying that the growth of investment slowed down. There must be an underlying reason, which cannot have been part of the plan.

It seems probable that the causes are associated with a sharp rise in military expenditures. The defence vote in the Budget increased from 9.4 thousand million new roubles in 1959, and 9.3 thousand millions in 1960, to 13.9 thousand millions in 1963. It seems probable that the sharp rise in the defence vote in 1961 led to a diversion to military use of considerable resources originally destined for civilian investment purposes.

Various "planned" investment projects had to be slowed down or abandoned, and so the output which they would have contributed to the national economy was not forthcoming. This must have had cumulative effects. These were exacerbated by a tightening of central control over investment, also dating from 1961 and surely no coincidence. Such controls follow a bureaucratic logic of their own. We may be sure that they halted some investment projects for which both labour and materials were available but which were considered of a non-priority category, while some priority projects elsewhere were halted for lack of labour or materials.

In the last years of Khrushchev's rule, this negative trend was strengthened by his insistence, in the context of a strained investment programme, that chemicals should be given absolute priority. This affected both the disposal of domestic resources and the import programme. The expansion of the chemical industry was pressed forward at too rapid a pace and, although the economy benefited from this (admittedly much-needed) development, such gain was in all probability outweighed by the losses inflicted elsewhere by cuts in the investment programme.

LABOUR SHORTAGES

One resource which has been particularly scarce is labour. The working population has been increasing rather more slowly than usual in recent years, owing to the impact of the war on the birth-rate — there were relatively few births in the years 1943–48. Thus, while in 1952–53 there were 15 million children aged 12–14 years at school, by 1956–57 the number had fallen to 7.4 millions. The numbers entering the labour force in the period after 1957 must have been unusually small.[2]

The precise effect of this on the size of the working population, however, has been "disguised" by the habit of giving annual statistics only of "workers and employees" employed by State organs and State enterprises, omitting most peasants. Until 1961, the reduction in the size of the armed forces was a compensating factor, but this seems to have been checked or reversed.

One industry which suffered particularly was building. In the

[2] However, the post-war births "bulge" is now beginning to enter employment. Recent press reports of unemployment relate in the main to married women (especially in Siberia), but also to smaller towns where no industrial expansion has been planned. Some enterprises are compelled to retain redundant labour. Soviet critics deplore the absence of labour exchanges to enable surplus labour to be systematically transferred to where it is needed.

two years 1959 and 1960 the size of the building labour force rose by 15 per cent. In the three years 1961–63 the increase was less than 2 per cent (in total, *not* per annum). True, the number of labour-saving machines in the industry increased, but no faster than before. On the contrary, there was a marked slow-down in new investments in the building industry itself: the increase in 1961–63 over the 1960 level was only 5 per cent (again in total). In view of the dependence of any investment programme on building, this, too, is a factor to be considered in identifying the causes of the slowing down of growth.

Further analysis of employment statistics by area and by industry merely serves to underline the difficulties. The largest increase in the labour force seems to have been in trade, catering, procurements and supplies (over 17 per cent in the three years 1961–63). Much of this was due to a very necessary improvement in distribution and catering facilities, but the labour so used meant other purposes were deprived. Workers in the fields of both health and education also increased in number rather more rapidly than in industry, where there was a rise of just 12 per cent in the three years. There was no sign of any substantial reduction in the farm labour force that might have relieved the stringency elsewhere in the economy.

There is also evidence of "geographical" difficulties. Thus several Soviet sources have pointed out that, while the plan envisaged an above-average increase in investment and in industry in the eastern half of Siberia, in fact the workers have "voted with their feet." Statistics show a net migration *out* of the area in question, for which there appear to be perfectly good reasons. It seems that the difference in wages is quite insufficient to compensate workers for the poorer housing and amenities, and for somewhat higher prices. Since a worker is, nowadays, free to leave any job or area, he moves, creating headaches for planners.

In addition to these various considerations, the period 1957–63 say a progressive reduction in the length of the working week.

HIGHER CONSUMPTION

Another factor of some relevance in any discussion of Soviet economic growth is the changed political climate and its effects on planners' priorities. Under Stalin, any conflict between the plan and the wishes of the citizens could be resolved by invoking the police, and a higher rate of investment could have perhaps been maintained by cutting consumption. In these respects there is now much less room for manoeuvre.

Symbolic of the changed situation was Khrushchev's decision to spend large sums in gold and dollars to buy wheat after the exceptionally poor harvest of 1963.[3] He himself publicly contrasted this policy with Stalin's: the latter, he alleged, would have continued to export grain. Maybe so. Certainly Stalin would have maintained imports of capital goods, and therefore of investment, at higher levels. Khrushchev's action is therefore a striking example of a sacrifice of investment to current consumption.

It should be added that, in actual fact, consumption has not increased at all rapidly in the past few years. Housing plans were not fulfilled; investments in agriculture fell significantly below planned levels; supply of textiles grew very slowly, and the re-equipment of light industry was slowed down.

All this, however, does not seem to have been deliberately planned. It seems that some of the present difficulties arose because of attempts to do too much (a predicament not unknown in Western countries). Although there was a disinclination to cut consumption and housing plans, paradoxically the resultant strains and shortages led *ad hoc* to the reassertion of traditional priorities.

OUTPUT OF INDUSTRIAL PRODUCTS

It must be stressed that the rate of growth in the output of many basic industries and fuels has remained high, and, apart from a shortage of coal in 1964 (due apparently to miscalculation), demand for such products has been met. . . .

[There is] a long list of consumer durables, in which, as a category, the U.S.S.R. is very far behind America, but whose output has grown rapidly in recent years (except for some items, including watches, cameras and sewing machines, for which the domestic market appears to be saturated).

. . . [I]t would be [therefore] foolish to speak of crisis and stagnation. Growth continues. Yet there is a sense of deep dissatisfaction with the functioning of the Soviet planning system. Partly this is due to the slow-down in growth, partly to the fact that output is failing to match requirements, and partly also to the audible creaking and groaning of an overworked and inflexible planning mechanism.

It is becoming increasingly evident that the old methods and organizational forms are a barrier to efficiency, at a time when a resumption of more rapid growth-rates requires more rational forms

[3] It may well be that shortage of currency arising from these wheat purchases caused the reduced Soviet purchases from Britain in 1964.

of resource allocation. The frank and hard-hitting debate which Soviet economists have been conducting in public and in print takes these propositions for granted. The problem is seen as one not of deciding whether radical reform is necessary, but rather of choosing the best, and least risky, from a number of proposals.

We must now define the nature of the malaise, trace its relationship to the deceleration of growth, and consider the various remedies proposed. There are two closely connected kinds of problems. The first, independent of persons and policies, is inherent in the system itself. The second stems from actual errors or decisions, taken especially by or under Khrushchev, although many of these resulted from attempts to deal with difficulties which were already there regardless of Khrushchev's will or actions.

DIFFICULTIES OF CENTRALIZED PLANNING

A good deal has been written on the subject of the strain to which the centralized planning system is necessarily subjected as the economy grows larger and more complex, and the point is perhaps too familiar to dwell on at length here.

It was part of the essence of "Stalinist" planning that the centre determined priorities, and that these priorities took precedence over criteria of profitability and local interests. It followed, logically, that the success criterion of all subordinate enterprises and authorities was the fulfillment of the central plan, i.e., obedience to instructions. The centre collected information about needs, found what resources were available, and, on this basis, decided which needs it would be possible to satisfy and what production and investment decisions were called for. The various organs of the administration then subdivided and broke down the plans in detail, so that in the end every enterprise (other than those of purely local significance) received orders about what to produce, to whom to deliver the products, from whom to purchase materials, how much to pay out in wages, and also plans for profits, costs, staff establishment, capital repairs, and so on. In the absence of an "automatic" mechanism for registering demand — more or less provided by a market (however imperfect) in Western countries — only the planners at the centre could aggregate and analyse information about what was wanted, where and by whom, and decide on the relative urgency of this or that requirement. Prices played a largely passive rôle, being inflexible and not even theoretically related to relative utilities or scarcities.

This meant the conscious planning and co-ordination of many

millions of interconnected decisions by many administrative offices. As the economy grew, and the simple priorities of Stalinism were diluted, this placed an immense burden on the planners. There was evident danger of lack of coherence, of inconsistencies between decisions taken at different levels and in different offices. The sheer size of the country, and the existence of fifteen federal republics, each with some decision-making powers, further complicated the process of planning, the more so as republican powers were somewhat increased after 1955.

Until 1957, each sector of Soviet industry was under a separate ministry (e.g., ministry for coal, for chemicals, for ferrous metallurgy, etc.). This "ministerial" system led, however, to "empire-building." Each ministry set up its own supply system, manufactured many of its own components, procured some of its own materials, pressed its own investment plans on the overworked co-ordinators of *Gosplan*. This caused wasteful duplication and unnecessary cross-hauls. In 1956, it led to the adoption of a five-year plan (the sixth) which had to be abandoned only nine months after it had been unanimously approved by the Party Congress, an unprecedented event — it was explained that the plan was not internally consistent. Indeed, it was not until 1959 that there was another long-term plan formally operating.

In December, 1956, Khrushchev's political rivals endeavoured to cope with the problem by setting up a super-ministry of economics, under Pervukhin, and subordinating the industrial ministries to it. By March, 1957, the political balance had swung the other way, and Khrushchev sought to solve the same problem by abolishing the industrial ministries, basing the process of planning and administration on over a hundred regional economic councils (*sovnarkhozy*), to which all industrial enterprises of significance were henceforth subordinated. This was intended to destroy the ministerial "empires." *Gosplan* was to ensure the proper co-ordination of regional plans.

CONSEQUENCES OF 1957 CHANGE

Experience has shown that the consequences of this decision were increased confusion and irresponsibility. There were two interconnected reasons for this.

First, the burden of central co-ordination proved too much for *Gosplan*, causing a proliferation of all-union State committees of various kinds, some with sector responsibilities (though with little executive authority), others with the task of co-ordination. By 1963, it proved necessary to set up a super-co-ordinator (The Supreme Council of National Economy) to co-ordinate the co-ordinators. Powers to allocate materials and to take production decisions were centralized again *ad hoc,* and regional councils and republican planners were often by-passed, further complicating lines of administrative responsibility. This was a logical consequence of a built-in and fatal weakness of the entire "regionalization" reform.

This weakness has been implied by the preceding analysis. In the "traditional" Soviet form of planning — sometimes described as planning for a "command economy" — only the centre has the information which enables it to judge the consequences of decisions made, say, at the local level. The regional officials did not and could not have such information, in the absence of any system by which the producing enterprise or region could judge the state of demand for their output or products. The sole effective criteria of regional decision-making were the orders of the centre. In the absence of such orders, there was bound to be a strong trend towards regional autarky.

To restrain this, to impose not only the centre's own priorities but also some degree of coherence in the allocation of resources, the centre had constantly to intervene. Otherwise, essential materials and components would be, and were, diverted from users located outside the given region. This "localism" (*mestnichestvo,* as it came to be called), was due not to any desire on the part of local officialdom to exalt local above national needs, but rather to the fact that their contribution to the national plan was judged by their fulfilment of the regional plan. Consequently, they allocated resources to facilitate the fulfilment of *their* plan, without knowledge of, or interest in, the consequences to other regions. It is this situation which compelled recentralization. For the record, I did, in fact, forecast this development within a few months of the promulgation or the 1957 reform.[4]

However, the resultant multiplication of planning authorities led to the second grave weakness that followed the 1957 reform. This concerns the effect of the change on the position of the managements of different enterprises. The powers of management were not in fact increased, although there was much talk of doing so. However, the simple lines of subordination of the "ministerial" system were disrupted.

Before 1957, an enterprise was under its ministry, from which it received all orders and plans; but after the reform, its nominal "boss"

[4] *Problems of Communism,* No. 6, 1957.

became the regional economic council. Output and material allocations were planned, at the centre and in republics, by large numbers
of organizations, basing their activities on products, not enterprises.
If, therefore, a given enterprise made, say, six products, it would be
likely to have six masters. This, in practice, meant that it had no
master, no one effectively responsible for planning the proper utilization of its capacity. So to the, perhaps unavoidable, errors inherent in
"command" planning were added those due to a faulty organizational
structure. For this, Khrushchev must bear some personal responsibility. The resultant muddles in supply and planning arrangements
were most vividly described by a senior official of the Kazakh republic,
who produced a diagram showing lines of subordination crossing and
criss-crossing, like a web spun by a drunken spider. No wonder there
was pressure for a more orderly planning system.

NEED FOR LESS CENTRAL CONTROL

The question of how best to reform an evidently faulty administrative
machine became entangled with another issue, with which it is closely
connected. This is to free the administration altogether from certain
tasks, by increasing the autonomy of enterprises through permitting
contract and negotiation on a customer-producer basis.

Some argued that the errors and inconsistencies of highly-detailed
administrative planning could not, in fact, be eliminated by reorganization. As long ago as 1959, Liberman, later to become more famous,
wrote in the party's fortnightly, *Kommunist,* that the complexities
"would overwhelm any apparatus of *gosplans* and supply-disposal
organs." Liberman and his fellow-reformers argued that the basis of
any solution lies in finding a way of greatly reducing the "command"
element in Soviet planning. They pointed out that the traditional
methods encouraged directors to strive to be given a modest plan,
since their success would be measured by its fulfilment; that a multiplicity of "plan indicators" led to inconsistencies, and put managements into the position of having to decide which of the mutually
exclusive orders had to be obeyed; that production plans should be
based on the requirements of the users, as directly communicated to
the manufacturing enterprise, and not on aggregated and global plans;
and that the attempts of managements to fulfil global plans (in tons,
roubles, etc.) led to undue emphasis on particular products, neglect of
quality, and to quite unnecessary waste. The avoidance of muddle at
factory level, the encouragement of initiative on the part of management, the reduction of the burden on the planners, all needed a

criterion by which the operation of enterprises could be judged, a criterion other than obedience to orders. Liberman and most other reformers, though disagreeing on matters of detail, agreed that such a criterion could only be profit, and that this meant a reform of the price system.

At this point, some readers may demur. All this talk about planning difficulties and confusion in making decisions does not square with evidence of progress in industry, space research and so forth. But there is really no conflict.

Some branches of Soviet industry benefit from the characteristic features of centralized planning. The planning of output, determining what goods should be produced, arranging for raw material and other supplies, all this is easier in some industries than in others: for example, in steel, coal, electricity, cement and oil. Even in many Western countries such industries are nationalized or controlled by monopolistic corporations. It is, therefore, not entirely coincidental that these industries have continued to do reasonably well in the U.S.S.R. As for space research, or weapon systems, these things depend not on free markets, competition, or rational prices, but on the quality of research staffs, and on the ability of the authorities to make available the necessary human and material resources. This the Soviet government can undoubtedly do.

The system, however, is quite evidently not able to cope efficiently with those sectors of the economy where there is a multiplicity of choices, or products, or raw materials, or ways in which resources can be used. One such sector, notoriously, is agriculture. As many Soviet commentators have pointed out, the continued deficiencies of this branch of the economy have adversely affected the supply of materials for industry and of food for the population, not to mention the balance of payments. Agricultural plans are seldom, if ever, fulfilled, in striking contrast to the achievements in manufacturing and extractive industries.

AGRICULTURE

The question of the shortcomings of agriculture can be most easily considered by taking various headings.

Under-investment

A substantial increase in investment in the period 1953–58 was followed by a marked slow-down of the rate of increase, in agriculture even more than elsewhere. Thus, between 1953 and 1958 investments in agriculture (in money terms) more than doubled, but in the following five years 1958–63, the increase was less than 50 per cent. This was far below the needs of this much-neglected sector, and meant shortages of many kinds of machinery, of fertilizer and of such elementary equipment as threshing floors, storage capacity and repair shops, to name only a few items. Rural roads are usually shockingly bad, with the traditional Russian spring and autumn *bezdorozhiye* (roadlessness) cutting farms off from the outside world and from their neighbours for months on end.

All this is well known, and no serious Soviet expert would deny it. It is a question of making the necessary resources available to set right the results of decades of neglect, when top priority was given to industrialization.

Status, Rewards and Attitudes of Peasants

On most collective farms the peasants still receive no guaranteed minimum pay or even a firm share of the gross income of "their" farm. Uncertainty as to their reward, plus the fact that there was some fall in average pay in the period 1957–62, has acted as a disincentive.

Peasants devote much effort to their tolerated private activities — a vegetable plot and a limited number of livestock — and to the sale of private produce in a legal free market. To combat the resultant loss of labour time on the collective farm, the authorities recently again sought to restrict, obstruct and tax these private activities. This has caused resentment and even some kind of spontaneous strike. Thus, a Soviet writer has described the refusal of peasants to go hay-making when they could use only 10 per cent of the hay for their own livestock, but how they worked hard when (under the influence of drink) the head of the farm ignored orders and promised them a third of the hay.

There is also deep dissatisfaction with peasant status. The denial to the peasant of the internal passport makes it difficult for him to move to town, and he is also discriminated against in respect of social benefits, although a recent decree did at last give collectivized peasants a right to an old-age pension.

Errors of Policy and Effects of Centralization

As long ago as 1955, Khrushchev himself denounced the practice of telling farms exactly what to do. He well knew that agriculture, by reasons of its infinite variety, is least suitable to bureaucratic orders. He said all this again in March, 1964: farm managements should be free, according to the rules, to adapt their activities to local conditions, subject only to meeting delivery quotas to the State.

Yet, in practice, Khrushchev used the party machine to impose from above drastic and repeated changes in the crop pattern and even in methods of cultivation, as well as in the number of livestock which farms were to have. The list of his campaigns is long, and protests against them, sometimes in print even during his political lifetime, have been loud since his fall. There was the maize campaign, which led to grossly excessive sowings in the wrong areas, regardless of climate, of availability of labour or of machinery, or of the wishes of management. There was the campaign for a great expansion of the number of livestock, although fodder supplies had not increased after 1958, with the result of falling yields of milk and a run-down in grain reserves, which had its consequences when bad weather led to a poor harvest in 1963. There was the campaign against sown grasses, oats and fallow, that led some local officials to outlaw valuable crops such as clover. Under the stress of successive campaigns, there was neglect of "non-priority" parts of agriculture, causing shortages of hay, potatoes, millet, and many vegetables. On top of all this, there were serious irrationalities in agricultural prices.

Once again, Soviet experts would doubtless agree that this is a true picture of the recent past, that must have adversely affected production. It is an interesting question, beyond the scope of the present article, to inquire *why* these deviations from good sense occurred, when the ill-effects must have been well-known, not least to Khrushchev himself.

Supply Inadequacies

Clumsy methods have been (and are) used to allocate materials and equipment. Farms have to accept the machinery and fertilizer which the authorities send them, whether or not it is what they need or have ordered. Building materials and all kinds of spare parts are often quite unobtainable. Some of these troubles may be related to the over-precipitate abolition, in 1958, of the State-run machine tractor stations, which at least had proper repair facilities and a permanent staff of technicians, as well as the supply priority possessed by a State organization.

Gigantomania

Despite warnings from experts, officials pressed for amalgamation of farms until, to cite a Soviet critic, they sometimes became so big that "any kind of operational management and efficiency in organization of production became not just difficult but quite out of the question."

To these various causes of the shortcomings of agriculture must be added, finally, the very real difficulties resulting from natural conditions or "Acts of God," if one may use that term in a Soviet context. The 1963 harvest was exceptionally bad, the 1964 harvest was very much better, but these were just short-term effects of bad and good weather, rather than evidence of a basic change in agricultural performance.

THE NEED FOR REFORM

Thus the slow-down in growth, and the strains which have been evident in the Soviet economic structure, have been due to a combination of factors. Some could be described as inherent in any system of centralized planning, some were due to human error or organizational inadequacies, some to the impact of military expenditure.

The need is increasingly felt to adapt the system to meet the requirements of the customer more flexibly, to relieve the intolerable pressure on the planning mechanism, to achieve more efficient utilization of resources. Any forecast of the future growth and shape of the economy must, therefore, depend greatly on what kind of reform is finally adopted. It must depend also on whether or not military expenditure is likely to increase. The present tough American policy — coming at the same time as the substantial loosening of Moscow's control over communists outside the U.S.S.R. — underlines the extent to which the Soviet leaders can no longer determine the international climate, which might severely limit any possible economies in military expenditure.

What chance is there of sensible reforms being adopted? The cry has gone up that they represent "revisionism," almost a return to capitalism or at least to NEP (the "New Economic Policy," a form of mixed economy which flourished in 1921–27). Some of these comments, whether they come from Washington or from Peking, seem well wide of the mark.

First of all, reform *must* come. It is necessary, and the necessity is understood by the party leaders as well as by economists. Indeed, the former have criticized the economists for failing to put forward agreed and practicable proposals, and one of the obstacles to change is precisely that reformers are busily arguing with one another.

The essence of *any* reform must be to replace the elaborate system by which a total of wants is determined — the fulfilment of which

then becomes the alloted task of various industries and enterprises —
by a system based on direct contractual relations between producer
and customer. It is (at last!) understood that the organizational forms
could be very different in different branches of the economy. As
already indicated, in some industries the existing system works reasonably well, and in these the retention of a considerable degree of centralization would be rational. In other instances, national, regional
or local groupings of enterprises will emerge; and, just as in the sub-
units of large corporations in the West, there will be various degrees
of autonomy for plant management. Far-reaching experiments are
being made with several hundred enterprises and groups of enterprises
left free to determine their own production and financial plans, subject
to the twin criteria of increases in profits and in total sales. This is an
adaptation of the proposals made by Professor Liberman, which have
been argued about for several years.

MISTAKES OF PLANNERS

Is this a departure from Marxism? A Soviet economist, L. Leontiev,
mocked *The New York Times* for asserting that the Soviets regarded
as "bourgeois" the conception that "the needs of the consumers and
not the decisions of bureaucrats" should decide what should be produced. Some in the West think that "decisions of bureaucrats" — or
planners' preferences — diverge in principle from the needs of users.
But do they? Certainly, the share of investment in the national
income, and also the general pattern of development and the priorities
involved in it, are matters of political decision in the U.S.S.R.

But do planners, *in principle,* wish to substitute their own preferences for those of the consumer in such matters as the design of
clothing, quality or style of shoes, or in a choice between expanding
output of refrigerators or of radiograms? When there is a difference
between what the consumer wants and what is actually available,
surely this is due in most cases to error or ignorance? If the creation
of direct commercial links between customer, retailer and manufac-
turer leads to closer conformity between what is produced and what
is demanded, why should this lead to a departure from "planners'
preferences"? Planners surely do not "prefer" a situation in which
materials are wasted in making unsaleable goods, while customers
queue for what they really want.

The same is true of relations between industries. A recent issue
of *Ekonomicheskaya Gazeta* told a sad story of how a dyestuffs factory
was working at 60 per cent capacity, producing the wrong dyes,

because its plans were based on anticipated requirements communicated to it several months before the textile factories (who use the dyes) were told of their production programme. Yet "without getting the agreement of dozens of offices the [dyestuffs] factory is not empowered to change the plan." Owing to the multiplicity of planning organs involved, "it is virtually impossible to find out who is guilty" of the errors. The resultant useless output and wasted capacity is the effect of wrong decisions by bureaucrats. Only bureaucratic vested interest could stand in the way of any reform which would make dyestuffs production conform more closely to user needs. Vested interest of this kind is not by any means unimportant, and it also applies very much to the various activities of the communist party machine. But this is not to say that Marxist theory or basic ideology are major obstacles to change. Nor is the use of profits as a criterion of the performance of an enterprise "un-Marxist," given that the profits do still belong to the State and not to the management.

Experiments are also being undertaken in the use of econometric techniques, computers, programming, as aids to planning. Soviet mathematicians are of very high quality. Many obstacles of a practical nature stand in the way of the widespread incorporation of mathematical techniques into planning, and it is clear that the computer will not be a substitute for the necessary decentralization measures of the "Liberman" type. Yet an improvement in planning methods, and some greater efficiency, should result from the work of the mathematicians.

The resistance of the ideologists has been overcome, and the victory of the new methodology has been formally "sanctified," by the award of a Lenin prize to the three men who did most to develop and to legitimize the new trends: the late Academician Nemchinov, Kantorovich and Novozhilov.

The Brezhnev-Kosygin leadership has repealed some of Khrushchev's more misguided measures. Within the party and in agricultural planning, his organizational reshuffles have been abandoned. Restrictions imposed in recent years on private agriculture have been lifted; there is to be a sharp rise in agricultural investments and also in prices paid to farms. Khrushchev's agricultural campaigns have been condemned in detail and as a technique, and farms have been promised much greater autonomy. The chemicals investments programme has been scaled down to reasonable (though still ambitious) proportions. These and other similar measures have been reasonable and sensible. They have been accompanied by business-like, sober speeches, emphasizing the end of "subjective" crash programmes and the unsound measures of the individual (unnamed!) who ran affairs until October 15th of last year.

WHAT ROLE FOR PRICES?

Yet, naturally, many controversial and unsettled issues still remain. The measures to enlarge the autonomy of individual enterprises in industry and in agriculture, with a larger rôle assigned to profits, call for a radically new approach to prices. Previously tolerated irrationalities become intolerable. How, then, should price control operate? How much freedom should there be to vary prices by negotiation? How many decisions on production and allocation of resources should reflect market conditions? How far can autonomy be granted to individual enterprises before throwing out of gear the entire mechanism of central control over the basic proportions of the economy? After all, one cannot realistically envisage a "free market" in current output and central control over investment decisions, when a sizeable share of current output consists of investment goods.

So there is uncertainty about how much "commercial" freedom it would be safe to grant, how many physical planning powers should remain at the centre, what mechanisms the centre should use to exercise control. There is argument about the effect of such reforms on growth and on the necessity for imposing political reforms on growth and on the necessity for imposing political priorities in the allocation of scarce resources. The reorganization measures, as and when decided, are bound to affect personal ambitions of ministers and of senior officials. Then there are immediate issues about priorities. The agricultural programme is very expensive, and other claimants on scarce resources will have to suffer cuts. In view of all this, it is entirely proper that the new leaders are taking their time, experimenting, carefully feeling their way, and perhaps disagreeing among themselves.

FUTURE PROGRESS

What progress is likely during the next five years? A five-year plan for the years 1966–70 is now being drafted, and may be published at about the same time as this article. Clearly, the declared intentions of the Soviet planners are an essential part of the basis of any serious estimate, which makes peculiarly hazardous any attempts at projections at the time of writing.

It may well be that the rate of growth in the national income will benefit from the remedial measures being taken in the agricultural sector, and also from a more rapid rise in investments generally. Soviet economists fear that, unless investment choices become more rational, increased investments will not yield a proportionate acceleration in production. This underlines the intimate connection between the prospects for the economy and the adoption of effective measures of reform in the planning system. These reforms, however, may cause confusion and misallocation in the short term, as the economy adjusts to a new and hitherto untried basis of operation.

Another point to bear in mind is that improvements in quality, and in the degree of satisfaction of wants, are seldom adequately reflected in output and growth statistics. Thus, if tyres are made to last twice as long, and if, since fewer tyres would be made, the time so saved were devoted to more leisure, the *statistical* effect of this desirable development would be a fall of output. Similarly, the demand is for better and more durable footwear, whereas the "traditional" system encouraged growth of quantity at the expense of quality.

The wise man, in all these circumstances, makes no forecast. But it is quite proper to warn against underestimating Soviet economic potential, and to express the view that there will be some limited recovery in growth-rates under the new management.

PART FOUR

DEVELOPING AREAS PLANNING

DOUGLAS S. PAAUW

Development Planning
in Asia*

The planning problems of Developing Areas are abundantly illustrated as Professor Paauw analyzes the changing techniques, orientation, and strategy of development planning in Asia. He distinguishes the various positions toward planning taken by countries within the area, and points out some difficult planning issues which affect the region as a whole. His article suggests some positive steps which would both improve planning and help to achieve more rapid growth.

Introduction

THIS BROAD, COMPARATIVE SURVEY presents the author's impressions of the state of development planning in the ECAFE Region.[1]

[1] The term "ECAFE Region" has come to be used in reference to those Asian nations presently associated with the United Nations Economic Commission for Asia and the Far East.

* From Douglas S. Paauw, *Development Planning in Asia* (May, 1965), pp. 3–29. Reprinted by permission of the author.

The central questions concern the extent to which development planning is currently involved in a dynamic process of improvement and the ways to hasten the application of methods for more effectively guiding the important long-run decisions that all less developed countries inevitably take, either consciously or by default. In this spirit, the paper focuses on questions related to what might be termed "absorptive capacity" for improvement in making development strategy and related decisions more rationally. The position taken is that potential for improvement must be judged in terms of initial benchmarks and conscious awareness among leaders in less developed countries of the *realities* of their specific situations. The attack on reality requires both a willingness to undertake frank (and often painful) self-evaluation and a capacity to discern what concrete steps must be taken at a particular juncture. Above all, it requires conviction that intelligent action is possible and the courage to act on this conviction.

It is important to remember that the step between perception of what needs to be done and the determination to act where political and social constraints are great is a very large one. . . .

Though they may lack the determination to act, most less developed countries have readily embraced the concept of development planning. In doing so, their motivations are obviously complex. While this is not the place to investigate this intriguing issue, it should be noted that planning agencies frequently have been established, and plans constructed, as a result of external pressures. In some cases, planning facades have been thought necessary as a condition for foreign assistance; in others, these facades have been constructed for national prestige reasons, when government leaders felt it was necessary for their nation to conform to a stereotype picture of the enlightened less developed country. Where such motives have impelled the development planning stance, national leadership has been inclined to give grudging support. Economic development is unlikely to become an activity of highest national priority, or to win broad support within the government, where a plan or plan organization is merely another piece of the accepted paraphernalia of new statehood.

. . . The central question is how to transform development planning into a realistic, new, and more effective approach to accelerate progress in developing countries. A large part of the answer must lie in the evaluations of planning efforts by the developing countries themselves. As a first condition for improvement, national leaders in less developed countries must develop an awareness of the gulf between present planning efforts and what might be done through determination, vision, and growing sophistication. Present misconceptions must be disavowed; hyperbole must be scaled down to realistic capabilities; and the planning process must be moved from the periphery to the center of government activity.

In this context, the present survey represents an effort to evaluate both planning practice in the ECAFE area and the current state of Asian thought on Asian development planning. Progress in ideas must certainly precede improvement in actions, and among many countries in the ECAFE region there is a strong tendency to criticize the past development planning experience. We find a new willingness to take a fresh look at concepts and theories, and even ideology, in terms of their relevance and usefulness in promoting social and economic progress. This is likely to lead to a growing awareness of the significance of the type of issues raised above. . . .

I. Commitment to Planning

The ECAFE area covers a large number of less developed countries which vary considerably in size, economic endowments and economic potential, and pre-conditions for development, and national goals. Virtually all countries in the area have national development plans; moreover, there is a general attachment to the principle that economic development is an important national goal. Yet, there is wide variation in the role that development planning has assumed. In many countries of the area, development planning continues to be a rather elusive concept; aggregate national plans may have been drafted and promulgated, but they have little impact in terms of policy changes or execution of investment programs. Similarly, among the ECAFE countries, the involvement of governments and the dedication with which they support national planning show the widest disparity. Despite existence of formal plans, development planning in most countries does not represent a determined national commitment to accelerate economic development through rational and coordinated policies. Progress toward building development planning into a process having a pervasive and positive impact on growth dynamics in these societies has been very meager. Hence, it is not surprising to find that as development plans have mushroomed throughout the area during the past decade, growth rates have generally fallen and with few exceptions they have lagged behind plan targets.[2] In the ECAFE

_____

[2] For evidence of the general decline in actual growth rates between the 1950s and the early years of the present decade, see ECAFE Secretariat, *Development Planning in ECAFE Countries in the Recent Past—Achievements, Problems and Policy Issues*, E/CN.11/CAEP.2/L.3, mimeographed paper prepared for the Conference of Asian Planners, Bangkok, September 24, 1964, Table 1, pp. 7–8.

area there is a growing awareness of this paradox and Asian planners are exploring the question why development planning has brought so little success. There have been expressions of chagrin at the disappointing performance in the ECAFE area during a period when other developing regions appear to have done better. Considerable discussion at the 1964 Conference of Asian Planners was addressed to this point. Yet, much of the growing self-criticism has not yet penetrated to the heart of the difficulties that have prevented development planning from becoming a strong stimulant to economic growth and development. . . .

THE DEVELOPMENT PLANNING LEADERS

When viewing the ECAFE area as a whole, one cannot fail to identify two countries, India and Pakistan, as exceptional in terms of their commitment to development planning and in the scope and quality of the national effort that is being brought to bear on economic development problems. In these countries, aggregate plan formulation is now being done with relatively sophisticated techniques. There is a growing effort to link aggregate plans with sectoral and project breakdowns and to emphasize action programs, although this should not be taken to imply that these problems have been successfully solved. Given their size and complexity, these countries confront and will continue to face serious problems of implementation, project control, and progress reporting.

The feature of Indian and Pakistani planning which has greatest importance for the ECAFE area, however, is the growing accent on continuous evaluation and revision of planning. In both countries, these nascent evaluative processes have been addressed to issues of plan targets and planning methods, as well as questions of development strategy. This new stance of flexibility has meant a healthy retreat from dogmatic positions as they become recognized as obstacles to effective planning. In both countries, relatively drastic shifts in major plan priorities, tantamount to significant changes in development strategy, appear to be resulting in more realistic and effective development programs. The adoption of an increasingly flexible and realistic approach to planning by two of the most influential countries in the region has not gone unnoticed among observers in countries where planning as a national commitment is less firmly established. . . .

Two examples supporting the point of growing flexibility in approach are cited here. In the Indian situation, the impact of continuous reevaluation on both strategy and method can be best seen in the departure from the rigid assumptions of the Mahalanobis Model which has long been the core of the Indian approach. The unrealistic presumption that the Indian economy could be adequately energized from the center through emphasis on the public sector with tight controls over private enterprise has been gradually relaxed. In the Fourth Plan, now in preparation, it appears that this Mahalanobis specter will finally be completely laid to rest. Indian planners appear to believe that the new plan will give forthright emphasis to promotion of the private sector as the major vehicle of growth in the Indian economy. The policy implications are likely to involve not only an emphasis on decontrol of private economic activity but also the search for additional ways to stimulate private initiative and agricultural expansion.

In the Pakistani case, it is noteworthy that a similar change in the government's attitude toward the private sector has begun to be reflected in planning.[3] But the example to which we point here concerns a new departure in policy to attempt coordination of plans with financial and fiscal policies, specifically, to raise the economy's lagging savings rate. Within the past two years, the government has moved to coordinate efforts by the Planning Commission with those of other relevant agencies to aggressively promote domestic austerity, simultaneously strengthening institutions to mobilize savings. While extreme caution is needed in interpreting the savings data,[4] it appears that the government's new policy, generated from experience, has had a dramatic impact on raising both Pakistan's marginal and average savings rates.[5]

Finally, in both India and Pakistan the support given by national governments to planning activities is unique among ECAFE countries. In both countries — in Pakistan more recently than in India — the government has come to provide unqualified support for planning activities. Albert Waterston observes that in the case of Pakistan, the transition from moderate government interest to strong support has been a key factor in strengthening planning functions.[6] This cen-

---

[3] Albert Waterston, *Planning in Pakistan*, Baltimore, 1963, p. 138.

[4] John H. Power, "Two Years of Pakistan's Second Plan," *Pakistan Development Review*, Vol. III, No. 1, Spring 1963, pp. 129–32.

[5] Power cites the Planning Commission's estimates presented in *Mid-Plan Review of Progress in 1960/61–1961/62 Under the Second Five Year Plan*, showing a rise in the average savings rate from 5.6 percent in 1959/60 to 7.4 percent in 1961/62 implying a rise in the marginal savings rate from 7.4 percent to 38.6 percent. Power, however, estimates the more recent marginal savings rate to have been 27 percent. Power, *op. cit.*, pp. 130–132.

[6] Waterston, *op. cit.*, pp. 133–134.

trality of the planning process has allowed an evolution from narrow public sector planning to an expanded role, including budgetary allocations, review and evaluation of plan implementation, and, as we noted above, a positive role in mobilizing domestic savings. Similarly, increasing political support has led to greater concern for the private sector, as well as efforts to integrate outlying regions more fully into the national development program.

THE SMALL EFFECTIVE PLANNERS

While planning in Malaysia and China (Taiwan) does not yet compare with India and Pakistan in comprehensiveness, sophistication, and national support, development planning in these countries shows real promise. In both there is a clear predisposition to lean basically upon private enterprise to provide the vehicle for economic growth and development. Hence, the role of planning is construed to be one in which the government will stimulate the growth dynamics of the private sector by providing social overhead capital, financial stability, and technical guidance, particularly for the benefit of lagging sectors in the economy. This realistic quality has imparted a problem-solving nature to planning activities of these countries.

In both cases, planning began by tackling problems at the micro-level and emphasizing the agricultural sector, with gradual progress toward establishing an aggregate planning framework. This bottom-up evolution has made problems of coordination between aggregate and micro planning less severe than in most other ECAFE countries where a top-down evolution is needed if coordination is to be effected. The pragmatic problem-solving approach has promoted the growth of a strong administrative structure to channel public resources into development projects with an emphasis on progress reporting, control, and close supervision of resource use.[7] It should be noted, however, that these structures have grown gradually from their basic ministry — or sectoral — emphasis. In Taiwan, the Joint Commission for Rural Reconstruction early became the core of development planning efforts, later joined by working parties from other parts of the government. It is only now, with the imminent phasing out of U. S. assistance, that serious thought is being given to setting up a strong central planning unit. The evolution has been more or less comparable in Malaysia with the now effective central Economic

[7] Malaysia had the advantage of an excellent administrative system, penetrating to the villages, developed to cope with security problems during the Emergency.

Planning Unit established for coordinating sectoral programs after sectoral planning had become well established, particularly in the Ministry of Rural Development. There may well be some significance in the fact that in both "small effective planners" the initial impetus came from experience and success in the rural sector.

The rural emphasis in early development activities has had a positive impact on promoting productivity in what might otherwise have continued to be a lagging growth sector. In Malaysia, government programs have stimulated growth in the agricultural sector through improving productivity in the major export crop (rubber) and opening new lands. The state has also promoted adoption of improved techniques to enhance efficiency in traditional small scale agricultural activities. In Taiwan, extension work and government assistance programs have significantly raised agricultural activity in both subsistence and export crops.

Recognizing the positive impact of these planned programs, government leaders in Malaysia and Taiwan have undertaken a commitment to more ambitious programs of development planning. As the tendency toward more aggregative planning has grown, however, the emphasis on relating aggregate planning to action programs has continued. In both countries there is concern with strengthening the link between projects, sector programs, and planning at the aggregate level; and in both there is a growing recognition of the importance of integrating development plans with annual budgetary operations. In Malaysia this process of evolution has produced what is undoubtedly the most effective system of progress reporting and project control to be found in any developing country.

THE FREE ENTERPRISE EQUIVOCATORS

The Philippines has toyed with development planning for almost a decade, having produced several plans, none of which have been taken seriously or implemented. Thailand is now in its first Six Year Plan. In both cases, planning has been a more or less academic venture with very little impact on decision making or action. Among the political elite generally there is a lack of feeling of urgency regarding development planning activities. In both countries, economic progress during the last decade has been relatively favorable, somewhere in the neighborhood of 6 percent per year in growth of aggregate product. Private enterprise has surged ahead to account for a substantial part of investment activity, while public sector activity has concentrated on providing investment in social overhead facilities

— the latter being a consequence of ministerial activity, however, rather than of coordinated central planning.

Development planning in these countries has made little progress because of administrative obstacles which have failed to be overcome in the absence of a determined effort by the national leadership to establish a planning process. In part, this equivocation appears to be due to the fact that no planning framework has been developed appropriate to the basically private enterprise nature of these economies. In both, the announced plans have been addressed basically to public sector activity, failing to incorporate the important private sector into the planning framework. This failure to adapt planning to the nature of these economies and the actual problems they confront has also been a major factor in preventing planning from obtaining widespread governmental and popular support. In this situation, the aggregate plans that have been produced have largely remained documents on the shelves of officials, providing little guidance to policy decisions or programs of action. Selection and execution of investment projects have been accomplished on an *ad hoc* basis, largely through ministries, completely divorced from the aggregate planning framework. Coordination of ministry programs has not occurred through either central supervision or the budgetary process. Ministry dominance over sectoral investment programs has been so complete that allocations suggested in plans have been defied openly, and this has been a major factor in preventing plans from becoming officially adopted. Yet, ministries are sorely lacking in trained personnel capable of translating sectoral programs into a consistent nexus of projects, or scheduling implementation on a systematic basis. Direction and supervision over these inefficient investment activities, such as a strong central planning agency might provide, are a prime need in the Philippines. . . .

The prognosis currently looks somewhat better for Thailand than for the Philippines. Following the collapse of efforts to implement effectively the Four Year Social and Economic Development Plan in the Philippines — signaled by the resignation of Sixto K. Roxas from the National Economic Council in early 1964 — a completely fresh start is needed. In Thailand, the current National Economic Development Plan (1961–66) has more or less survived, and a rather uncritical mid-term review, outlining the program for the second phase (1964–66) was recently issued.[8] This reevaluation is clearly cast in

8 National Economic Development Board, *The National Economic Development Plan, 1961–1966, Second Phase 1964–1966* (English edition), Bangkok, January 1964.

terms of sectoral (Department) surveys, and the lack of an effective aggregate framework is clearly apparent. Moreover, the sectoral programs do not appear to emphasize micro-planning of the kind that sparked improvement in the planning processes of Malaysia and China (Taiwan).

THE DOCTRINAIRE NATIONALISTS

If development planning has had an air of unreality in Thailand and the Philippines, the free enterprise equivocators, this is even more true for the doctrinaire nationalists among ECAFE countries — Ceylon, Burma and Indonesia. In these, a nationalistic socialism calling for widespread government ownership and control of economic activity has been espoused as an ideology. There has been considerable experimentation with development planning, with little impact on policy formulation, investment programming or economic progress.

In general, these societies have concentrated on revamping traditional economic and political institutions grafted onto them during their colonial experience. In the resulting political and economic instability, conditions have not been conducive to the spread of rational development planning. Institutions to mobilize and allocate investment resources either through markets or public decision have been destroyed or eroded; they have not been replaced with effective new mechanisms to discharge these important development functions.

In another interpretation, planning has been so imbued with political overtones that the technical and institutional aspects of planning have suffered. Ideological and political diversions have caused these societies to utilize inefficiently their available supplies of technical personnel, their existing economic institutions, and even their existing economic capacity. Similarly, "plans" in these countries have had an unusually high political or noneconomic component. This has meant that an important, in some cases a dominant share of resources mobilized for public allocation has been used for purposes that have not raised productivity or output.

The doctrinaire nationalistic approach in these countries has appeared to have an adverse effect on economic incentives. Private sector performance has been sluggish and public institutions set up to replace private activities have not operated with efficiency adequate to offset the reduction of private initiative, entrepreneurship and management. During the past five years, over which the disavowal of rational approach to economic policy has been most apparent in these countries, growth rates have dropped sharply in all three — falling to near zero for both Ceylon and Indonesia.

While there is, of course, considerable variation among these countries, in general it can be said that the doctrinaire approach has produced a widening gap between announced goals and achievements. There is a wide gulf between what national leaders appear to anticipate from their national economic programs and what can be achieved through reliance on the new and rapidly changing public institutions to control and direct economic activities. Lack of realism in assessing both resource mobilization potential and capabilities for transforming resources into output-increasing investment has been a major characteristic of their programs. . . .

II. Development Planning Issues

EVALUATION OF PAST EFFORTS AND PROGRESS

Throughout the ECAFE area there is now a deep concern about the region's mediocre growth performance in the recent past, the relative ineffectiveness of development planning, and the implications of these setbacks for the future.[9] National leaders in most of the ECAFE countries are acutely aware of the fact that these countries as a group have the world's lowest level of per capita income. They view with alarm the fact that, in general, the ECAFE countries have realized low growth rates relative to other developing areas, and that growth rates have shown a tendency to fall below those achieved during the 1950 decade. There is an awareness that Asia holds a major share of the world's population, and that the area has been experiencing the world's highest population growth rates.

Other aspects of inter-regional comparisons also trouble Asian planners. ECAFE leaders note with concern the fact that progress toward establishing regional cooperation to promote development efforts in their area is lagging behind progress in Latin America and Africa. In this sense, there appears to be a clear demonstration effect from other regional groupings of less developed countries to spur nominal or real efforts for improving ECAFE performance. . . .

[9] The discussion of development planning issues is based primarily upon the author's participation in the Second Conference of Asian Planners, Bangkok, October 1964. The Conference was attended by delegates from 16 Asian countries (including Iran), from 6 Western countries and the U.S.S.R. Two countries, Israel and West Germany, participated in a consultative capacity. Substantive items in the Conference agenda were three: (1) progress and problems in planned economic development; (2) long-term macro-economic projections for countries in the ECAFE region; and (3) approaches to regional harmonization of national development plans.

The Secretariat's paper, presented to the Second Conference of Asian Planners on the subject of past failures and successes,[10] addressed itself to a review of the traditional bottlenecks to development. Major emphasis was given to the continued importance of domestic savings and foreign exchange as bottlenecks to rapid economic growth in most ECAFE countries. In the most positive section of the paper, the Secretariat put considerable stress upon lagging growth in the agricultural sector as a major factor depressing growth throughout the region.[11] This theme became dominant in the Conference discussion concerning past failures. The Conference Report places strong emphasis on the importance of "a resurgence of the agricultural sector," pointing to such critical areas of action as incentives, extension services, land reform, and overhead capital to enhance agricultural productivity. The problem of labor unemployment and its correctives was noted in passing in the Secretariat review, while key factors in planning having to do with organization and entrepreneurship were touched upon with caution. . . .

AGRICULTURE VERSUS INDUSTRY

On the one hand, the prevailing view among Asian planners appeared to be that the specific issues should be settled on the basis of individual country characteristics, with regard to development priorities generally. On the other hand, there was no apparent disagreement with the ECAFE Secretariat position that priority should be given to improving agricultural productivity both by expanded investment and by improved incentives. The Indian delegation observed that this was more true for India, given the massiveness and inertia of its agricultural sector, than for any other country in the region. For this reason a substantial increase in investment inputs in agriculture is anticipated during the Fourth Five Year Plan.

The lesson which development economists have just begun to learn — that is that a developing economy cannot grow rapidly without support from its agricultural sector — appears to have also been learned in the ECAFE region. On the other hand, there was some disagreement about the wisdom of concentrating on agricultural development at the expense of industry, on the basis of relative comparative advantage — a position advanced by Thailand and Nepal.

[10] ECAFE Secretariat, *Development Planning in ECAFE Countries in the Recent Past—Achievements, Problems and Policy Issues.*

[11] "It is now generally agreed that it is the poor performance of the agricultural sector which largely explains the failure of most economies of the region to grow as rapidly as desired." *Ibid.,* p. 51.

In addition to the general issue of priorities for agriculture, there was considerable interest among planners at the Conference in the specific measures appropriate for agricultural advancement. Extension services to involve farmers in an action program were emphasized by China (Taiwan) where such efforts have had spectacular success. Notable in this regard was the stress placed upon incentive systems appropriate to stimulating agricultural output, a problem which has been largely neglected in the past throughout much of the ECAFE area. Even the Soviet Union's delegation concurred on this point.

THE PRIVATE SECTOR

On the issue of the role of the private sector in the development planning process, Indian planners also made a strong plea for a more liberal and realistic approach. The position advanced was, in essence, that democratic planning involves reliance upon the private sector in the largest possible measure. This positive new stance toward the private sector will apparently be built into the Fourth Five Year Plan by stepping up the volume of assistance given private development efforts and by attempting to improve incentives for private entrepreneurship.

This is obviously a major issue in development strategy, and general support for the Indian position seems to suggest that the dogmatic socialist strain which has characterized so many past planning efforts in the ECAFE area is on the wane. There was no dissent from the Indian point of view. Rather, strong support was given to the principle of stimulating all components of mixed economies. In this connection, the emphasis on invigorating the private sector was reinforced by repeated reference to widening the scope of the plan impact. The case for linking central planning to widespread community activities and sparking maximum public participation was received with considerable enthusiasm.

If this new Asian thinking — and it should be stressed that this was the dominant *Asian* position — is followed by action, development strategies embodied in plans are likely to be substantially revised in countries other than India. Until now, virtually all Asian plans have had an unduly strong public sector bias, and nowhere has planning for private sector development been seriously attempted. There is great danger, therefore, in the possibility that shifts in emphasis will be precipitous. Here, too, zeal to implement a new philosophy may quickly outstrip capacity to effectively alter actual policies and programs. The writer's apprehension arises partly from the apparent gulf — at the present stage of Asian thinking — between endorsing a new broad approach and the specific policies and methods appropriate to realizing the approach. Little attention was given to the problems implicit in efforts to more effectively incorporate private sector activity into development plans. As noted below, discussion concerning long-run projections showed a tendency toward unreal abstraction, and the goal of using projection techniques to set and implement targets for the private sector was completely ignored. Similarly, problems of institutional arrangements to maximize the positive impact of central programs on private investment and output were not broached. In fairness, however, it should be pointed out that it may be premature at this point to discuss the substance implied in the new approach sweeping the ECAFE region. Considerations of this type may be raised at the next stage of the discussion.

If these impressions are correct, current ECAFE experience points to this general area in development planning as one which should be accorded highest priorities in research work. Even in advanced countries, the art of coordinating public sector plans and private activities is undeveloped. There is urgent need to adapt existing methods quickly and to devise new ones, if ECAFE planners are to act successfully upon their current impulse to broaden the scope of planning by maximizing the extent to which private sector activities are involved in the planning processes.

AUTARKY VERSUS COOPERATION

The Asian region has moved with great caution on the matter of regional economic cooperation. In the past the essence of regional cooperation has consisted of periodic consultation through international meetings, supplemented by a few joint development projects involving neighboring countries. The chief example of the latter is the Mekong River Project affecting the four riparian countries.

In recent years, the ECAFE Secretariat has encouraged more direct efforts to enlarge the scope of regional cooperation, and participating countries have shown some response. The Asian Institute for Economic Development and Planning was proposed by the first session of the Conference of Asian Planners in 1961, and became a reality in 1963. The Ministerial Conference on Asian Economic Cooperation, meeting in Manila in December 1963, authorized first steps toward establishing an Asian Development Bank. It is likely, however, that final agreement on a Regional Bank will take considerable time, since the political problems that must be resolved are both complex and delicate. On the other hand, the demonstration effect pressures from other regions already possessing a functioning Regional Bank are having a perceptible impact in prodding positive action.

The deeper issues concerning regional cooperation are just beginning to be explored by Asian planners. These issues involve patterns of long-run development strategy, the extent to which country autarky will be checked and country specialization promoted to expand potential intra-regional trade among the region's developing countries from its present low level.[12] The ECAFE Secretariat proposals to promote greater regional cooperation strongly favored emphasis upon harmonization of production plans by sector as the first priority.[13] It was argued that trade liberalization alone would have little effect in expanding regional trade, since the structures of ECAFE economies tend to be more competitive than complementary. . . .

Despite some degree of concurrence on the principles of regional industrial development, there is considerable dissent from the ECAFE Secretariat position with regard to agriculture, particularly food products. The Secretariat paper pointed to the threats which food self-sufficiency drives posed to traditional rice exporters and also emphasized that expansion of food in deficit countries might be uneconomic in terms of alternative uses of resources. Asian planners, by and large, tend to reject this approach. There is a dominant view that countries are entitled to do as much as possible to encourage progress toward self-sufficiency in foodstuffs. The Indian position on this issue is that the prime importance of improving agricultural productivity dovetails with the necessity to avoid continuance of an onerous foreign exchange burden associated with food shortages. Given the pervasive new stress on revitalizing agriculture, therefore, ECAFE planners are loath to view programs to achieve self-sufficiency in foodstuffs as autarkic. It should be noted that this philosophy poses serious threats to achieving a viable pattern of specialization and trade among ECAFE countries. It is clearly inimical to the long-run interests of those countries which, being relatively efficient in the production of foodstuffs, choose to exploit their present comparative advantage in trade. On the other hand, it is reasonable to doubt that food self-

---

[12] Intra-regional exports among the developing countries of the ECAFE region in fact declined from 26.2 percent of total exports in 1952–54 to 22.5 percent in 1960–62. ECAFE, *Approaches to Regional Harmonization of National Development Plans in Asia and The Far East,* Bangkok, September 1964, p. 9.

[13] *Ibid.*, especially pp. 13–30.

sufficiency intentions in some countries will actually bear fruit in the near future.[14]

THE ROLE OF FOREIGN ASSISTANCE

Asian planners, by and large, represent the view that foreign assistance has an important role to play in development programs. They recognize that the countries showing most rapid growth in their area have received large amounts of foreign assistance. There is also a growing conviction that foreign assistance must be more carefully woven into domestic planning to accelerate country self-help efforts. The Indonesian view that foreign assistance has many drawbacks apparently receives little overt support among Asian planners in non-Communist countries. In the current Indonesian view, substantial dependence on foreign aid for development momentum places recipient countries in a vulnerable position. This implies independence from foreign assistance as a policy objective.

Foreign assistance is viewed by Asian planners generally as critical in terms of the total foreign exchange requirements of development programs. This implies a prevailing view that in the ECAFE region the foreign exchange bottleneck is a more serious obstacle to development than the domestic savings bottleneck. Yet, there is awareness of the limitations to foreign capital inflows resulting from domestic absorptive capacity. While there is some resistance to the notion that foreign assistance should be tied to the finance of particular development projects, the failure of many countries to generate a flow of suitable development projects is viewed as a matter of great concern.

In addition to underlining the capital component of foreign assistance, Asian planners see an important role for technical assistance. Priorities in this connection appear to include assistance in planning itself, especially in plan implementation and evaluation techniques, assistance in improving data for planning — a problem which received considerable emphasis at the Conference of Asian Planners — and assistance for developing training programs for personnel involved in all aspects of planning, particularly those concerned with plan execution.

---

[14] In the case of Indonesia, for example, an intention to become self-sufficient in food within one year was reiterated at the Conference. Realistic assessment on the basis of past performance, however, suggests that only gradual reduction of food imports will actually be possible.

LONG-RUN ECONOMIC PROJECTIONS

Most less developed countries of the ECAFE region have prepared long-run projections in connection with one or another of their economic plans. In addition, the ECAFE Secretariat has recently issued its own projections of long-run growth for 10 countries.[15] Reviews of these efforts by both the Secretariat and a working party of experts were presented to the Conference of Asian Planners to serve as the basis for discussion.[16]

The ECAFE Secretariat put forth the view that, since long-run projections are designed to assist the development planner in formulating development policy, "extrapolation based on the coefficients or structural relationships derived from the past time series will be far from adequate.[17] Following this observation, a strong case is made for "policy oriented" projections, in the context of a model which clearly distinguishes among target variables, structural coefficients, policy instruments, and exogenous elements.[18] The Secretariat paper presents two alternative projection models (one a Harrod-Domar type and one a more typical Keynesian type). Alternative country projections were developed from the application of these models, in most cases employing both past and modified parameters, the latter including the presumed impact of policy changes. In reviewing the Secretariat findings by country, the expert working party compared these with country projections (where available) and in some cases added their own revised projections. This bewildering assortment of long-run projections for many countries was presented to the Conference with differences in assumptions clearly specified in most cases, but — almost inevitably — with inadequate justification for any particular set of assumptions.

It might appear that Asian planners were suddenly confronted with an embarrassment of riches, with many sets of long-run growth projections for several ECAFE countries. In the judgment of the present writer, however, the opposite is true. Many factors contribute to this unsatisfactory state of long-run projections for ECAFE coun-

[15] Burma, Ceylon, China (Taiwan), India, Indonesia, the Republic of Korea, Malaysia, Pakistan, the Philippines, and Thailand.

[16] ECAFE "Review of Long-Term Economic Projections for Selected Countries of the ECAFE Region: Report by the Fourth Group of Experts on Programming Techniques," E/CN.11/CAEP.2/L.4; and ECAFE, "Review of Long-Term Macro-Economic Projections for Selected Countries of the ECAFE Region, Addendum," E/CN.11/CAEP.2/L.4 Add. 1.

[17] *Ibid.*, Addendum, pp. 3–4.

[18] *Ibid.*, p. 4.

tries, but chief among them is clearly the lack of depth of the presently available estimates.

The problems of the quality of these projections can be reduced to two general categories. In one category are problems of methodology, a matter of applying projection models that are not well adapted to the special features of each economy. In this regard, the ECAFE attempt to evolve a standard ECAFE model may be viewed as more of a hindrance than a contribution to improved growth projections. If a case could be made for the application of a standard model, with minor adjustments for country applications, question would then have to be raised as to whether or not the ECAFE model is the "ideal" one for the entire region. Several features of the most generally applied ECAFE model, the Harrod-Domar type,[19] would appear to disqualify it for this role. First, the ECAFE model contains no explicit savings function, employing rather a Keynesian type consumption function. This obscures the savings policy considerations, making it virtually impossible to incorporate within the model savings behavior assumptions where this might be done if relevant data and analysis were available. Yet, the ECAFE Secretariat singles out the domestic savings problem as one of the two most critical, continuing obstacles to growth in the region. Secondly, with regard to the other major bottleneck stressed by ECAFE, i.e., the shortage of foreign exchange, the ECAFE model is also weak on both the export and import side. Most economies of the ECAFE region are heavily involved in the world market, showing high ratios of exports to total products. Yet, the ECAFE projection model gives no explicit recognition to this important role of exports; they are not built into the model in a functional way. Moreover, it is difficult to anticipate terms of trade and to make allowance for their effects. Similarly, on the import side, the model operates with a general relationship between imports and total output while it is unlikely that such a behavioral relationship exists in most of the ECAFE countries. Finally, given the high rates of population growth in the area, it would seem desirable to view growth requirements in terms of per capita income and consumption objectives. The ECAFE model, however, is formulated exclusively in terms of aggregate growth targets.

To put the argument in another way, the aggregate projection

---

[19] There was agreement among participants at the Conference of Asian Planners that the other ECAFE projection model, the Keynesian type, was inappropriate for the less developed countries of the region. The leader of the discussion on this subject, Professor Jan Tinbergen, took the initiative in expressing this view.

models currently used in the ECAFE region fail, with few exceptions, to formulate the critical relationships in such a way that policy conclusions are directly apparent. This is due in part to the fact that, given data capacities of most less developed countries, it is not possible to go beyond aggregate projection models with only the broadest structural relationships. Despite this limitation, however, some degree of adapting the model structure to emphasize an economy's most pressing development problems is possible. In Indonesia, for example, where the level of production has been closely related to the volume of raw materials and spare parts imported, the ECAFE model's formulation of the production function in terms of a direct capital-output relationship is obviously misleading, at least in the short-run.

Given problems of this nature, one may legitimately question whether efforts devoted to producing a variety of alternative projections with slightly differing assumptions make the best use of available talent. It would appear that intensive country studies are needed to improve the quality of projections, first, by providing information to guide the construction of the most appropriate projection model, and secondly, by providing improved estimates of the critical parameters in the resultant model. This brings us to the second category of factors that have impeded progress toward better long-run projections in the region — those having to do with underlying data.

It will be apparent from the discussion that many discrepancies in results among available long-run projections for ECAFE countries may be accounted for by the variety of alternative guesses about parameter values, their sensitivity to policy measures, and assumptions that policy decisions of one kind or another will be made. Here we stress an almost intuitively obvious point; differences of this kind can only be settled by intensive country studies, concerned not only with improving basic data supporting estimates of aggregate variables, but also with providing a basis for judging the likelihood and feasibility of major policy decisions that will have one or another effect on important determinants of long-run growth. . . .

III. Conclusions

It is apparent . . . that the status of planning in ECAFE countries and the major issues that now occupy the minds of Asian planners are inevitably related. The issues focus more upon basic questions of development strategy than techniques of planning. The technical planning questions — even the basic problem of long-run projection methods most appropriate for guiding planning decisions — are regarded as matters of importance in very few countries of the ECAFE area. Development planning experience in most ECAFE countries has not yet made such technical problems relevant. In the few countries where there has been a serious commitment to development planning, however, there is a realization that planning methods must be improved to guide policy decisions more efficiently and to improve the achievement of plan targets.

By and large, however, the issues still concern the underlying strategies most appropriate to accelerating economic growth in the ECAFE region. There is a growing awareness that development must involve the entire society; the easy assumption that public sector activity could open the way to rapid industrial growth, pulling along the whole society, is in process of being reluctantly discarded. Much has been learned from the experience of India and Pakistan — and from Communist China's planning reverses as well. In particular, ECAFE countries show an increasing concern with the importance of relying upon agriculture as well as industry and upon private as well as public activity to provide a forward momentum in their economies. In most ECAFE countries the more practical difficulties of harnessing national resources to energize their total societies are yet to be aggressively tackled. These difficulties will come to the fore if and when development planning institutions become a new center of gravity.

When the more practical stage of determined action is reached, important planning issues that now appear to be neglected will be uncovered. Chief among these is the problem of explicitly taking into account the area's rapid rate of population growth. Development requirements must reckon with these high rates of population growth if the low levels of per capita income and consumption are to be raised. Planning in these terms will lead to another neglected aspect of prime importance — the matter of raising domestic savings rates through practicing greater domestic austerity. In the absence of concrete austerity policies and measures in most ECAFE countries, average savings rates have remained stable or have fallen during the past decade. A major issue concerns the sources from which developing societies will mobilize the needed increases in domestic savings. Present thinking in most countries of the ECAFE region goes little beyond recognition of the savings bottleneck; attention has not yet begun to focus clearly upon the necessity of adopting strong programs of action to substantially raise both domestic savings and the capacity to absorb them productively. Foreign capital assistance will contribute to progress toward self-sufficient growth only after these basic internal problems are resolved.

Finally, despite substantial progress in a few ECAFE countries, integration of plans and action is still one of the region's most neglected problems. A major lesson from Malaysia's and Taiwan's experience is that emphasis on action programs can be effective in widening the impact of planning within a society as a whole. This suggests that efforts to strengthen project execution and control, ministry by ministry, may be a means to the end of inculcating the planning habit on an increasingly broad scale. Similarly, an emphasis on building planning and progress reporting into capital budgets may well pave the way for gradually expanding the time horizon for planning annual allocation of resources to lengthening periods. Progress in moving downward from aggregate plans to guiding action at micro-levels has proceeded so slowly in the ECAFE area that pressures generated by wide participation are needed to make planning meaningful and effective in an area where disappointing performance has focused critical attention on the whole process.

RAYMOND VERNON

Comprehensive Model-Building in the Planning Process: The Less-Developed Economies*

Professor Vernon in his essay distills from his first-hand experience of planning the more important lessons which the past can teach us. His emphasis on the habit-changing, exhortative function of planning, the divergence of action from plan, and the importance of cultural and social factors is timely and germane. Hopefully, future planning will benefit from learning past mistakes.

* From Raymond Vernon, "Comprehensive Model-Building in the Planning Process: The Case of the Less-Developed Economies," *The Economic Journal*, Vol. LXXVI, no. 301 (March, 1966), pp. 57–69. Reprinted by permission of *The Economic Journal* and the author.

IT IS ONLY a decade or so since economists have learned how to set up and manipulate comprehensive models of a national economy. And it is only a decade or so since the less-developed economies have begun to turn to national planning as a means of helping them to achieve their economic aims. The two activities have now flowed together, intermingled, to a degree which sometimes makes them appear indistinguishable to laymen. Yet they are clearly separable concepts. Among planning practitioners, the questions whether and how comprehensive model building supports the national planning function are a source of endless debate. The task we have set ourselves here is to explore the extent to which national planning and comprehensive model-building are congruent activities for the less-developed countries with market economies.

If one had been writing of "national planning" before the 1950s one might have been referring to nothing more than a general commitment to rational analysis as a preliminary to governmental action of some sort; in this loose sense, national planning included a requirement for analysis with respect to all types of national economic policy: monetary, fiscal or trade policy; public or private investment; or any other economic area in which a governmental policy is required.

Little by little, however, the phrase has come to mean something a good deal more specific. According to the emerging norms, no country can be said to engage in national planning unless it has a well-articulated plan whose contents satisfy certain minimum criteria. Such a plan has to offer much more than a general statement of national goals, as in the path-breaking Sexennial Plan of Mexico presented in 1934. It must satisfy at least two requirements: comprehensiveness and consistency. For comprehensiveness, it must explicitly state a set of output and income targets; and it must trace out in quantitative terms, the path between these targets and the necessary inputs, such as investment, foreign exchange and labour force. For consistency, the standards are more permissive. There may be consistency tests between the composition of the goods produced by the economy's various sectors and the composition of the goods demanded by those sectors; between the saving implied by the model and investment required by it; between foreign-exchange income and foreign-exchange expenditure; between public income and public out-go; between goods flows and money flows; between the quality of the labour force needed and the quality of the labour force to be supplied; and so on.

In the past few years another major conceptual advance appears to have been shaping, soon perhaps to become still another prerequisite for an adequate plan. According to the new concept, a national plan must not merely be demonstrably comprehensive and consistent in all its parts; it must also make the best possible use of a country's scarcest resources, whatever they may be. Accordingly, the acceptable plan may be tested in the future not only by the standards of comprehensiveness and consistency but also by that of optimality.

Of course, in a field as new and as vital as national model-building nothing can be so simple and clear cut. In point of fact, the practitioners are locked in dispute on so many basic issues. Some of these differences have to do with the kinds of questions a model should be expected to answer; some relate to the methodology appropriate for the solution. Before we turn to some of these differences, however, it may be well to consider whether a model which purports to provide a comprehensive, consistent and optimal growth pattern is appropriate to the needs of national planning in the less-developed market economies.

THE PLANNING OBJECTIVES

To a considerable extent, the question answers itself.[1] One object of national plans is to promote national growth. National growth is hardly helped if the paths that are being pursued are internally inconsistent. A model which tested the internal consistency of a set of

[1] The pages that follow draw heavily on the field experiences of the Harvard Development Advisory Service in six countries and upon numerous published sources, including Everett E. Hagen (ed.), *Planning Economic Development* (Homewood, Ill.: Richard D. Irwin, Inc., 1963); also U.N. Conference on Science and Technology, *Organization, Planning, and Programming for Economic Development*, Vol. VIII in a series of papers prepared by United States contributors (Washington: G.P.O., 1962); Albert Waterston, *Planning in Morocco* (Baltimore: Johns Hopkins Press, 1962), and subsequent pamphlets by the same author on a number of other countries; Clair Wilcox, *The Planning and Execution of Economic Development in Southeast Asia, Occasional Paper in International Affairs No. 10*, Harvard University, January 1965; Louis J. Walinsky, *Economic Development in Burma, 1951–1960* (New York: Twentieth Century Fund, 1962); Albert O. Hirschman, *Journeys Toward Progress* (New York: Twentieth Century Fund, 1963), especially Chapter 4; John F. Lewis, *Quiet Crisis in India* (Garden City, N.Y.: Doubleday, 1964); R. S. Milne (ed.), *Planning for Progress* (Manila: Institute of Public Administration, 1960); papers of the United Nations Meeting of Experts on Administrative Aspects of National Development Planning, Paris, June 8–19, 1964 (mimeographed) and others.

development proposals would be a useful weapon indeed. By the same token, a model which identified the optimal use of some scarce resource, such as foreign exchange, also could provide a great boost to national objectives.

All this is self-evident. What is perhaps less apparent is that the national plans which the less-developed countries produce are not intended simply to describe a path of development which is consistent and optimal. The reasons why governments go through the difficult and complex business of the drafting and promulgation of a plan are a good deal more complex.

The objective that is common to most countries in the drafting of a national plan is to justify a claim for foreign aid. It is a rare national plan produced by a less-developed country which fails to specify the existence of a resource gap to be filled by foreign assistance. In the ordinary case, if the first approximations of the national model failed to produce such a gap the growth goals of the country would be raised until a gap appeared. The national plan, therefore, is tested in the first instance for its ability to justify a foreign resource gap *ex ante* on lines best calculated to eliminate the gap *ex post*.

National plans have other purposes as well. They are promulgated by governments as a political document; as a rally point for the co-operation and support of the electorate, and as a generator of common hopes and expectations. To the extent that national plans have this purpose, the criteria of consistency and optimality, as the planning technician might define them, may often be irrelevant and may even be an outright hindrance.

Confronted with political realities of this sort, the characteristic reaction of the planner is a badly suppressed impatience. The reaction is understandable; but it is hardly defensible. In the first place, the politician's instinct may well be right; if economic growth is in fact to be achieved, popular support may be an indispensable condition, perhaps even more critical than a consistent and optimal plan. In the second place, the planner's claim to be able to provide an optimal solution (if he makes such a claim, which many do not) may be quite misleading. In the practice of model-building "optimality" must be measured by some simple index, such as the increase achieved in consumer-goods output or investment or gross national product. In reaching his solution, the planner does not purport to weigh such alternatives (when they *are* alternatives) as increased employment versus increased production, high savings rates versus egalitarian income sharing, public ownership versus private ownership, increased education versus increased consumption and so on. Yet issues such as these are at the heart of the national aspirations and national debates of the less-developed countries.[2]

One is pushed to the conclusion, therefore, that a comprehensive model of an economy which purports simply to develop and test the consistency and optimality of an economic strategy is at best only partially relevant to the country's needs. What is needed is a much more complex, more restrained, more qualified strategy, far more multivalent that the naïve meaning of "consistency" and "optimality" might suggest.

Does this conclusion rule out the use of model-building as an adjunct to national planning? Not at all. As we shall see later on, the use of models is not inconsistent with restraint, qualification and multivalence. The difficult problems for the model builder come from other directions. One of his more forbidding difficulties has to do with the acquisition of information in the less-developed economies.

THE PROBLEM OF INFORMATION

The process of planning in market economies, in the forms in which it has been developed so far, depends for its validity upon certain critical capacities. These include the capacities to gather up information and to create common planning assumptions among the sectoral planning agents. It seems trite to point out that an underdeveloped economy's capacities in these areas are utterly different from those of an advanced country;[3] and it may appear superfluous to observe that any planning process adopted by these countries must reflect the fact. Yet that painful platitude needs to be stressed in view of the evidence that it is so persistently disregarded.[4]

[2] The point is persuasively made in comments by Edward S. Mason at a National Bureau of Economic Research Conference on Economic Planning at Princeton, November 1964. The Mason comments were in reaction to a model elaborated by Richard E. Eckaus and Louis Lefeber, "Planning in India." Presumably the model and the reaction will eventually appear in an N.B.E.R. publication.

[3] For some cogent observations on the extent of these differences, see Burton A. Baker (ed.), *Public Administration, A Key to Development* (U.S. Dept. Agriculture Graduate School, Washington, 1963), especially the papers of David E. Bell and Roberto de Oliviero Campos.

[4] Planning methodology as taught in the development institute of the Economic Commission for Latin America and its sister institutions in Africa and Asia does not yet differ very much in content from the methodology taught in analogous institutions in France, Holland and Sweden. The object of planners in most less-developed countries — an object from which they are only half-heartedly dissuaded by visiting experts — is to borrow the processes of Yugoslavia or France or Holland, as the case may be.

"In all countries," says a United Nations expert report, "the experience of planning shows that information does not flow in a single direction and that the flow between the center and the periphery is a dynamic process, a dialogue which represents a reciprocal enrichment."[5]

This, of course, is the description of an ideal, not of a state of being. In actual fact, in most of the less-developed countries of the world "a dialogue" of the sort envisaged is very rare indeed. The important channels of communication are better suited to monologue . . . [A]nyone who has been exposed to the inner processes of governments in less-developed countries usually comes away with a feeling of disjointedness and disarticulation, with a sense of separate members moving without much relationship to one another. The planner who is trying to weigh the effects of his money allocations to the various public sectors is so remote from the sensors and doers of the public sector that his information flow-back has only a slight relation to reality. The engineers in the Ministry of Communications and the supervisors in the Ministry of Education continue peacefully in their accustomed rounds; either they are unaware of the ferment in the planning office or they are unwilling to be responsive to it.

If the exchange of information between the various bits of the public sector is inadequate for the planning of optimum resource allocation in the governments of the less-developed countries, the flow of ideas and information between the public and the private sector tends to be even less so. Not that businessmen and civil servants are wholly out of contact with one another. On a day-to-day basis, individual businessmen in the developing countries spend a great deal of time soliciting the various ministries for import licences, permission to invest, exception from taxation and so on. But this is not the sort of communication that contributes much to the exchange of information relevant for planning. It neither widens the horizons of the cloistered planner nor sharpens the expectations and projections of the private operators.

The problems of bridging the gulf between the public and the private sectors are disconcerting in their difficulty. In the ex-colonial areas of Asia and Africa the civil service usually tends to assume the social mantle of the displaced colonial office and to regard itself as one of the more exalted sectors of the national structure. The prob-

[5] United Nations Meeting of Experts on Administrative Aspects of National Development Planning, Paris, June 8–19, 1964, *Administrative Aspects of Planning in Developing Countries* (report of a preliminary study, mimeographed, February 1964).

lem that this creates is heightened wherever the private sector is heavily represented by officers of international enterprises, or wherever it is represented by *auslander* groups such as the Lebanese and Indians in Africa and the Chinese in Southeast Asia. Communication across gulfs as wide as this is guarded and difficult. . . .

With such wide communication gaps between the planning apparatus of nations and the various executing and sensing organs of the economy, the possibilities of effective feedback of information from executors to planners and of digestion and assimilation of such information in the planning process suffer under grave handicaps. So planners are obliged constantly to engage in a game of blind man's buff, envisaging how the country might be if only they had the opportunity to see it. The choice of planning technique, if it is to be at all relevant, must take this fact into account.

COSTS AND YIELDS IN MODEL BUILDING

The multivalent purposes of the national plan place some severe limitations on the relevance of certain types of model-building; the unavoidability of large areas of ignorance restrains the planner even further. But beyond these two considerations, there are others as well. One of these is the cost — that is to say, the opportunity cost — of time and man-power used in constructing the model.

The cost of model-building depends more than anything else on the model's complexity. Though the most complex of them is really extraordinarily simple in conception, some models attempt to take more factors into account than others. The crudest and simplest growth model of all, for instance, may attempt to "explain" and predict the growth of an economy on the basis of population changes and savings rates. The more complex models, as we noted earlier in our introductory observations, may weave a more intricate course; these may distinguish the output implications of capital inputs to different sectors, may trace through the interacting relationships among the various industries, may attempt to take account of different demand functions for different products, may try to account for bottlenecks in scarce factors other than capital and may build in various other assumptions of lesser or greater sophistication.

In view of the cost considerations, how comprehensive and detailed should a model be?

First, let us be clear that the costs are sometimes high. The really scarce commodity of the less-developed countries is usually trained man-power, especially man-power devoted to the business of government. The personnel involved in the development of a comprehensive model are usually those who otherwise could be deployed to questions of sectoral strategy, large-project feasibility studies, or trade, payment and monetary policy. The cost of diverting personnel from these fields has to be weighed against the gains to be derived from the model elaboration.

But what if this is so? Can the planner afford to be without a plan? Can the planner afford to take "avoidable" leaps to conclusions, jumping across an intervening gulf in which the values of many parameters are assumed and in which the internal consistency of a spectrum of conclusions is taken for granted? One must agree at once that there is great psychic pain involved in such a procedure, when the nature of the procedure is evident in all its nakedness. For instance, if some unsophisticated minister were to conclude that his nation could afford to build both a heavy steel industry and a heavy chemical industry in the same plan period, the planner who could see some way of testing the consistency of the minister's assumption would be greatly tempted to do so.

Before the planner decides to devote his time to a test of internal consistency, however, he should be crystal clear on exactly what he gains through the test. An analyst who was charged with testing the internal consistency of the conclusions of the unsophisticated minister might find that the minister's conclusions would be rendered consistent if one could bring oneself to accept the credibility of fairly high marginal savings rates, fairly low capital-output ratios, fairly large foreign aid assistance programmes and so on. However, the credibility of these assumptions is a matter of judgment, a reaction from the viscera. It derives from history and from analogy. Yet, in the end, as Kuznets has observed, its acceptance for projection purposes is an act of faith, not of reason.

The crime of the unsophisticated minister, therefore, is not that he has used his judgment. It is rather that he has used it too early, before voicing his assumptions in a form relevant to econometric test. Once his assumptions are articulated in acceptable form and his evidence has been marshalled, the debate shifts from whether the model is internally consistent to whether the assumptions of the model are plausible.

It is here that one should recall the limitations of growth models in general, and of growth models for underdeveloped areas in particular. There is no need to labour the point; too much has already been written about the subject. The extensive simplifying assumptions that have to be made in order to keep such models manageable

— assumptions of linearity, of homogeneity, of continuity — greatly dilute their value for normative or predictive purposes.

When we use such models for less-developed areas the short-comings grow more acute. *A priori,* there is strong reason to believe that history and analogy offer less reliable guides in the case of the newly developing areas than in the case of some advanced nations. Typically, the history of development in the underdeveloped areas is brief; typically, it is grossly and imperfectly recorded. Even if recorded with great accuracy, however, one would expect to find highly unstable and swiftly changing patterns at even modest levels of disaggregation.

In the ceaseless effort to deal with problems of this sort model-builders have begun to make increased use of "sensitivity tests"; that is, tests to determine the extent to which the results derived from a given model may be altered by changing any given exogenous element in the model. Tests of this sort can represent a considerable advance; they free the model-builder from the constraint of using a single value for any variable and permit him to try out a range. But they still do not free him from an onerous set of judgments: Where history and analogy offer little guide, what is the relevant range of any variable? And what combinations of ranges ought to be tested together? Is one justified, in the end, in reacting to the results of a model in which one assumes, in combination, a "very low" birth-rate, a "very high" savings-rate, a "very high" set of supply elasticities and a "very large" flow of foreign aid? Or should one's viscera be allowed to reject the results as improbable?

The question might seem captious if it were not for the fact that variables which may formally appear as exogenous and independent in a model may not be independent at all. Birth-rates, savings-rates and import propensities, for instance, may all be linked together; a "sensitivity test" for one variable at a time, therefore, may be inappropriate and irrelevant.

Sensitivity tests which link all the related variables appropriately can conceivably generate a wider range of results than those which test each variable one at a time. If the results cover a wide range a serious question is raised as to the utility of the model being tested. Alternatively, if they cover a narrow range one begins to wonder if the model has really captured the factors which are important for the economy's growth. Sensitivity tests, therefore, may prove more disturbing that reassuring.

So far, we have dealt with the problem of projection through model-building as if the issue were principally one of developing the best estimates of future parameters. If this were the principal problem one might be entitled to a reasonably optimistic view of the utility of the complex model. But there is another issue, much more deep-seated and — on the face of it — much more intractable.

Growth models are usually made up of a series of parametric relations: A units of coal plus B units of labour produce C units of energy; D added dollars of income generate E added dollars of saving plus F added dollars of consumption; and so on. The model-builder, of course, has no illusions about the invariant nature of the outcome. He is aware that A units of coal plus B units of labour may produce more or less than C units of energy in the individual case, depending on all kinds of controllable or uncontrollable, predictable or unpredictable, sources of variation. But the value C may be fairly representative, with deviations being relatively insignificant.

The difficulties become methodologically ominous, however, whenever the distribution of values for C can be expected to have a very large variance; and even more ominous when the distribution is expected to be badly skewed. In these cases C stands for less and less, and reliance upon C as a representative value involves more and more risk. Yet, in an underdeveloped setting, it is not unreasonable to expect distributions with large variances and considerable skewness to occur with disconcerting frequency. The expectation seems especially great when the parameter involved is one representing a capital-output ratio.

The reasons why one ought to anticipate a wide and greatly skewed range of performances in the capital-output ratios of underdeveloped economies are fairly evident. Such societies characteristically operate on slim margins of safety. An unanticipated breakdown of transport cannot easily be countered by bringing some other transport into action. An unpredictable run of faulty parts cannot be offset by drawing on emergency inventories elsewhere in the economy. The illness of a scarce specialist cannot be dealt with by calling on other repair men. In these departments the supply elasticities of the economy are close to zero. *A priori*, the capital-output ratios in such a situation would seem to range from slightly lower than "normal" to very much higher than "normal," with some cases of total failure recorded at the extreme right of the distribution.

If a unique value cannot be used without the risk of very large margins of error one of the fundamental assumptions in model-building exercises is raised in question. If one is obliged to state that a given input can generate a constellation of outputs with given probabilities the existing techniques simply cannot move very far towards

a solution without bogging down. It may be that the most efficient way of plotting a strategy of development ought not to begin with the question that is implicit in most models that are in current use, namely: Given a bundle of scarce resources, how best can they be put to use? The most efficient way of plotting a strategy may require a different kind of initial question, such as: Given a starting-point in the development process, what are the various paths that may be pursued through different combinations of strategy and different impacts from ignorance or random error?

The new question is easier asked than answered. Straight away, we are plunged into a field that is still in its infancy among economists: the field of decision-making under conditions of uncertainty and ignorance. The emphasis upon uncertainty and ignorance in the decision-making process is a familiar one in the military and business world, of course; and some scholars have made a little headway in formulating systematic approaches to such situations.[6] The interest of the businessman or the military strategist in formulating his problems in this way is evident. For one thing, he is constantly obliged to reckon the cost of acquiring new information against the risk of proceeding without it; he cannot take it for granted that the value of more knowledge exceeds the cost of its acquisition. For another thing, the businessman or the military strategist cannot rely upon the *mean* performance of any venture to serve as a basis for decision; he does not dare to lose sight of the fact that if, by purest chance, he should lose his capital or his troops in any venture, he might never be able to achieve a mean performance.

It is curious how few of these concerns have yet penetrated into the formal aspects of economic planning. While the literature on the economics of the firm deals extensively with the risk function of the entrepreneur, the literature on project and programme analysis in the field of economic development is practically silent on the problem of

[6] Writings in the field of decision-making under conditions of risk and uncertainty are by now very extensive. The best survey of the literature that has come to my attention is Joseph L. Bower, *Descriptive Decision Theory* (National Planning Association, October 1964, mimeographed). For a succinct summary of the literature covering the contributions from psychology, mathematics and economics in the period up to April 1960, see Ward Edwards, "Behavioral Decision Theory," in Paul R. Farnsworth (ed.), *Annual Review of Psychology* (Palo Alto, 1961), pp. 473–93. An interesting discussion in the context of capital investment, with a short bibliography stressing the contributions of the economists, appears in Jack Hirschleifer, "Efficient Allocation of Capital in an Uncertain World," in *American Economic Review,* Vol. LIV, No. 3, May 1964, pp. 77–85. In a quite different tradition, see G. B. Richardson, *Information and Investment* (Oxford Univ. Press, 1960).

risk.[7] For example, the conventional approaches to project and pro-gramme analysis in the field of public investment make no satisfactory allowance for degree of uncertainty of outcome. Yet intuitively, no one would disagree that as between two investments with the same expected outcome the investment with the smaller variance is more attractive. . . .

In sum, the main stream of national planning techniques may carry us a little way in plotting the growth of the underdeveloped areas; but it does not carry us very far. Its weaknesses stem from many causes. Part of the problem is the overly simplistic character of the relationships that present-day models are capable of handling. Accordingly, the best of such models cannot be expected to yield a great deal more than the simpler varieties. In part too, the techniques have limited utility because they demand so much projection of magnitudes which cannot accurately be projected. To be sure, the models change the point in the decision-making process at which bias, intuition and judgment play their role, and they force on the model-builder a more precise articulation of his bias. But they do not reduce by very much the scope or the play of these factors. Neither do they raise critical questions regarding the consequences that might ensue if, because of a run of unforeseen bad luck, a series of inputs should yield much less than the expected outputs.

THE PRACTITIONER'S GUIDE

In attempting to prescribe an optimising course of conduct for the practitioner in any institution, it is usually helpful to have some descriptive or normative theory of the institution well in mind. We do not have a theory of the behaviour of governments in under-developed countries, descriptive or normative; and we do not seem likely to acquire one.[8] Without pretending to any real theoretical underpinnings, however, one can still suggest an approach to model-building for the planning practitioner.

The practitioner in the field of planning, from the day he takes

[7] An outstanding exception is found in Arthur A. Maas and others, *Design of Water-Resource Systems* (Cambridge: Harvard University Press, 1962). See also Pierre Massé, *Optimal Investment Decisions* (Englewood Cliffs, N. J.: Prentice Hall, 1962, for the English translation), especially Chapter 8, "Problems of Economics of Uncertainty."

[8] Efforts to develop such a theory for an infinitely more simple institution, the business firm, seems to be making only the most laboured progress. See, for example, Richard M. Cyert and James March, *A Behavioral Theory of the Firm* (Englewood Cliffs, N. J.: Prentice-Hall, 1963).

up his task, is usually the target of two streams of demands: one is a series of demands that he should frame policies to meet the crises already in being, without waiting a moment to improve his knowledge and broaden his data; the other is the demand that he should develop a global long-term strategy that is comprehensive, consistent and optimal.

How the planner allocates his attention in situations of this sort seems to depend very much on his personality and prior training. A total disregard for short-run problems would be a denial of the Keynesian maxim, as well as a threat to the planner's prospects of being taken seriously by the powers-that-be. On the other hand, a total preoccupation with short-term problems could mean that no progress was being made in improving the base for meeting the next problem. In any case, total preoccupation with short-run issues would be difficult in light of the usual political need for a plan as a national rallying point, and the usual need of prospective lenders for a plan as an affirmation of the rationality and solid good sense of the lender.

As we have insisted throughout this paper, a plan which is "optimal" in the econometrician's sense does not necessarily fill these needs; and a plan which is "consistent" in that sense does not necessarily offer much more than the illusion of consistency. Accordingly, there is no overwhelming virtue in technically satisfying these requirements.

Looking back on the experiences of planners, the process seems to be one of satisfying the needs of the politicians and lenders in the early stages, with the use of "models" whose consistency tests are of so low an order as to add little to the demonstrated validity of any plan. Meanwhile, the planner uses the occasion of each short-term problem-solving exercise to justify the collection of data which could shed light on other problems. He uses considerable resources on data-collecting activities, therefore, but his data-collecting priorities are determined rather more by the short-term exigencies than the formal requirements of a comprehensive plan. Gradually, the circle of knowledge is widened by successive bites. In this kind of setting each decision is made with resignation to the fact that ignorance exists outside the circle of information and that the assumptions about other interrelated parts of the economy are less than comprehensive.

At the same time, however, while accepting ignorance and risk as inevitable ingredients in the situation, the planner is freed from the smothering constraints of the oversimplified model. He can more readily disengage himself from the assumption of linear functions if he feels the need; he can add subtleties to interrelationships which equations cannot carry; he can overleap patches of ignorance with intuitive leaps, if he is prepared to take the risk.[9]

Working in a few critical areas at a time, the planner pushes back the boundaries of ignorance as far as he can. Carried on over a sufficient period, a process of this sort generates a heavy statistical fall-out. Eventually it begins to reduce the cost of formal model-building. Little by little, formal comprehensive models of one sort or another can be used as an added check on the more subtle, more searching sectoral analyses. Eventually, the added cost of generating and manipulating complex formal models may be sufficiently small as to become a regular part of the flow of planning activity.

At that stage the problem of the planner in the use of the model is no longer one of cost: it is the risk of forgetting that the consistency, comprehensiveness and optimality of the planning decisions in the model are in good part the product of his own assumptions; and his own assumptions are likely to mask much of the bias, ignorance and uncertainty which the layman has so much more difficulty in concealing.

[9] A provocative description of the possibilities of blending Leontief inter-industry analysis with intuitional leaps and guesswork is presented in Hollis B. Chenery, "The Use of Interindustry Analysis in Development Programming," in Tibor Barna (ed.), *Structural Interdependence and Economic Development* (London: Macmillan and Company, Ltd., 1963), pp. 11–27.

PART FIVE

QUANTITATIVE ECONOMIC PLANNING

BERT G. HICKMAN

Quantitative Planning of Economic Policy*

No discussion of planning would be complete without some attention being given to developments on the frontier of technique in this rapidly advancing field. Professor Hickman, in this summary report of a recent Conference on the Quantitative Planning of Economic Policy held at the Brookings Institution, suggests some of the technical issues that affect the working planner. His discussion indicates how much has been accomplished, and perhaps more important, how much still remains to be done.

THE BASIC LOGIC of the theory of quantitative economic policy is set forth with admirable clarity in Henri Theil's paper. The policy problem is viewed as analogous to the theory of rational consumer choice, in which the consumer is assumed to maximize his utility,

* From Bert G. Hickman, *Quantitative Planning of Economic Policy* (1965), pp. 2–17. Reprinted by permission of The Brookings Institution.

115

subject to the budget constraint given by his income and the prices of goods and services. Thus to solve the problem of consumer choice, it is necessary to specify (1) a utility or indifference function, (2) a budget constraint function, and (3) a conditional maximization procedure. In the same way, to solve the policy problem it is necessary to specify (1) a preference function for the decision-maker, (2) a model of the economy setting forth the constraints facing the decision-maker, and (3) a conditional maximization procedure.

Now, in the pure theory the preferences and constraints can be given exact mathematical expression, and exact procedures exist for finding the maximum. In actual practice, the precision implied by the pure theory may possibly never be attained, but it is certainly a goal worthy of serious and diligent pursuit. Moreover, by laying bare the logical structure of the problem, the pure theory provides an indispensable set of concepts for systematic thinking about the methods and procedures of quantitative policy planning.

To give the theory operational content, Theil specifies a linear econometric model of the economy and a quadratic preference function. The econometric model describes the quantitative relationships estimated to exist between the economic variables under the control of the decision-maker (such as tax rates, government expenditure, and central bank holdings of government securities) and the noncontrolled variables which he is interested in affecting by policy actions (such as employment, the consumer price level, and the balance of payments). In this respect — the use of a linear econometric model of the economy — Theil's approach closely resembles the pioneering work of Jan Tinbergen, and the similarities and differences are worth noting.[1]

In Tinbergen's nomenclature, the controlled variables are the policy *instruments* and the noncontrolled variables representing policy objectives are the *targets*. Two other classes of variables also appear in a complete econometric model representing the macroeconomic structure of an economy. These are the exogenous variables or *data* which are taken as given by the policy-maker and those noncontrolled endogenous variables which are *irrelevant* to the policy decision even though they may be directly or indirectly affected by it. . . .

In policy applications neither Tinbergen nor Theil works with the complete structural model of the economy. Instead they eliminate the irrelevant endogenous variables by algebraic manipulations until

[1] J. Tinbergen, *On the Theory of Economic Policy* (North-Holland, 1952; 2d ed. 1963), and *Economic Policy: Principles and Design* (North-Holland, 1956).

they are left with a set of equations equal in number to the target (noncontrolled) variables, where each equation contains only one target variable and all other variables are therefore either instruments (controlled variables) or data.[2]

At this point the two men part company, since Tinbergen eliminates the maximization problem as such and instead assumes that the decision-maker has specified a fixed value for each of the target variables. The equations are then solved simultaneously for the set of values of the instrument variables which is consistent with the fixed targets and the given data. These are the values at which the decision-maker should set the instruments in an attempt to attain the specified targets, given the information at his disposal.

This procedure does not guarantee, of course, that the target values will actually be realized even if the instruments are set at the specified values. In the first place, the exogenous data are given, in the sense that they are not determined by the model, but they must often be forecast instead of being known with certainty. Secondly, the coefficients relating the instrument and target variables must either be estimated by statistical probability techniques or established by other empirical methods or *a priori* assumption; hence they are also not known exactly in any given application.[3] As C. A. van den Beld and and Tsunehiko Watanabe show us, both sources of error have proved troublesome in the policy planning experience of the Netherlands and Japan, and this is doubtless true in other countries as well. One of the virtues of econometric policy analysis, of course, is that it remorselessly exposes such errors, so that their causes can be analyzed and efforts can be made to reduce them.

Other salient characteristics of the Tinbergen approach may be summarized as follows:

1. The approach lays particular stress on the structural interrelationships of the economic system, thus driving home three important lessons: a change in one instrument variable will in general affect the values of all target variables; a particular target variable may be importantly affected by a change in an instrument variable with which it is related and indirectly through other endogenous variables, so that the best policy attack is often an indirect one; and a rational economic policy requires coordination of all important policy instruments in a unified program.

[2] The data variables are absorbed in the constant term of the model equation used in the simplified examples given by Theil in the present paper.

[3] In this approach the coefficients of the policy model will usually be derived from those of the structural model instead of being estimated directly, but the same remarks apply to the structural coefficients.

2. The approach reveals whether a specified set of fixed targets is *compatible* — in the sense that all the target values can be achieved simultaneously with the given set of instruments. *Incompatibility* can arise for two reasons. One, if there are fewer instruments than targets, the number of unknowns (instrument variables) in the policy equations is smaller than the number of equations, and a solution is impossible except by coincidence. Within the Tinbergen framework, this situation can only be corrected by increasing the number of instruments or reducing the number of targets until there is an equal number of each in the equation system. Two, even when a unique solution is possible because the number of instruments and targets is equal, it may turn out that one (or more) of the *boundary conditions* placed on the values of the instrument variables has been violated. Such boundary conditions constrain the permissible values of the instrument variables within certain ranges: e.g., tax rates cannot be increased more than x per cent or government expenditure varied by more than y percent within a particular time span. Boundary conditions may be imposed for technical, institutional, or political reasons. No matter what the reason for imposing it, if one of the instrument boundary conditions is violated in the original solution, it is necessary to modify the original set of targets, usually by substituting the violated boundary condition for one of the original targets, so that the former instrument itself becomes a target, and then to re-solve the system for a consistent set of instruments and targets. It may be necessary to try several modifications of the system before a consistent solution is found.

3. Should the number of instruments exceed the number of targets, the number of unknowns will exceed the number of policy equations, and an infinite number of solutions will usually be possible. In this case, arbitrary values can be chosen for a selected set of "excess" instrument variables and the system can then be solved for the remaining instrument values. This situation provides great flexibility insofar as instrumental choice is concerned, since it permits experimentation with alternative combinations of instrument values to attain the given set of targets.

Let us now return to the point at which Theil and Tinbergen parted company. Theil, instead of assuming a set of fixed targets, specifies a decision-maker's preference function that includes all instrument (controlled) and target (noncontrolled) variables, but does not depend on fixed values of the instruments or targets. Rather it is specified in terms of deviations of the unknown values of the instruments and targets from their stipulated desired values. Moreover, each deviation variable is weighted to show the relative importance attached by the decision-maker to a deviation of that particular variable from the level which would be desired for it unconditionally — i.e., if its attainment did not affect the other targets or instruments. The preference function is then maximized subject to the constraints given by the set of equations showing how the instrument and target variables are related in the econometric model of the economy. The solution gives the best attainable combination of target and instrument values, when account is taken both of the decision-maker's preferences with respect to goals and of the limits placed on his ability to achieve these goals within the economic system represented by the econometric model.

It may at first be thought strange that desired values of the instruments enter the preference function along with the desired target values. It must be remembered, however, that some instrumental variables also partake of the nature of policy objectives or targets in their own right. An obvious example is government expenditure, which may be desired for its direct contribution to well-being, in addition to its indirect effects on private investment, employment, and other potential target variables. Moreover, even when a particular instrument has no direct welfare connotations, to restrain its movements may be desirable for political reasons or because of economic considerations that are not directly incorporated in the macroeconomic model. Incidentally, worth noting is that Tinbergen's procedure of imposing boundary conditions on the values to be taken by the instruments is analogous in important respects to the inclusion of weighted deviations of the instrument variables from their desired values in the preference function and can accomplish much the same results.

Several conceptual advantages may be cited for the preference-function approach over the method of fixed targets. First, a unique solution is obtainable irrespective of whether the number of instruments exceeds, equals, or falls short of the number of targets. Second, the substitution of flexible for fixed targets not only adds realism to the specification of policy objectives but makes it possible to find an optimal decision without disregarding any of the targets, whereas under the Tinbergen approach one or more targets must sometimes be dropped to obtain a consistent solution. Third, when a quadratic preference function is specified, the important problems of uncertain predictions and of decision-making under dynamic conditions are easily handled, as Theil's paper will show.

The simplicity of the approach as set forth by Theil is admittedly largely a result of the assumption of a quadratic form for the preference function. It is this assumption that permits use of the certainty equivalence theorem and results in simple linear decision rules for the maximizing policy strategy. The principal conceptual deficiency of the quadratic form is that it treats positive and negative deviations from the desired values as equally undesirable, whereas asymmetric preferences are doubtless realistic for some targets and instruments — the decision-maker must surely prefer for example, that the employment target be missed on the high side rather than on the low side. Any particular mathematical specification of the preference function can of course only approximate reality; therefore, on an operational level, the important question is whether the quadratic approximation is more appropriate than other workable alternatives, and this can only be discovered by systematic empirical research.

POLICY MODELS AND APPLICATIONS

For rigorous application of either the fixed-target or preference-function approach, a complete econometric model must be built, in which all relevant target and instrument variables are included and all coefficients are numerically estimated. The 36-equation model currently used by the Dutch Central Planning Bureau . . . is an excellent example. It is an annual model, designed for short-term macroeconomic forecasting and the planning of short-term stabilization policy.

Although it is true that great progress has been made in the improvement of such models since the pioneering efforts of Tinbergen in the early 1930's, this is still an active research area with many stimulating challenges. Much of the progress is due to the development of Keynesian economics, which provided an ideal basic framework for these short-term models, relying as they do so heavily on aggregative variables drawn from the national income accounts. By the same token, however, the Keynesian concepts would be largely empty of empirical content were it not for the great strides that have been made in the definition and measurement of national income and product within a consistent and increasingly elaborate social accounting system. Another vital contribution has come from the elaboration and refinement of sophisticated methods for the specification and estimation of functional relationships in econometric models — a difficult technical field which the complementary papers by Jati K. Sengupta and by Fox and Thorbecke ably survey. Finally, the modern electronic computer has reduced the computational cost of estimating and manipulating large equation systems to practicable proportions in both time and money.

In contrast to The Netherlands, both France and Japan have focused their planning procedures primarily on long-term development objectives rather than short-term stabilization goals. There is a corresponding difference in the principal techniques of quantitative economic analysis. Instead of the closed, short-term macro-econometric model that is the central feature of Dutch planning, the French and Japanese planning bureaus rely principally on long-term projections and input-output tables for the empirical analysis of economic constraints.

The principal characteristics of the long-term (five- or ten-year) projections, which provide the basic framework for the French and Japanese plans . . . is to project GNP and its components for several alternative potential growth rates and to examine the feasibility of the alternatives in the light of the constraints involved on both the demand and production sides, after which one of the alternative projections is selected to serve as the planning framework. Again, we find heavy reliance on the Keynesian income-expenditure theory and the national income and product accounts, just as in short-term macroeconomic models. In contrast to the short-term models, however, in which the existing size of the labor force is usually the only specified production constraint, it is necessary in projecting long-term development paths to give explicit attention both to the availability of labor, capital, and materials inputs over time and to the rate of productivity advance.

The functional relationships in these long-term projection models are generally simple in form and are not as a rule estimated by sophisticated statistical techniques. Numerical values are assigned to the parameters by such devices as historical trend analysis, average observed saving propensities and capital-output ratios, input-output tables, and estimates of informed persons or firms about particular sectors. This is not a static intellectual field, however, and examples are given in the papers by Cazes, Shishido, and Watanabe of the constant search for better structural specifications and improved methods of parameter estimation and consistency analysis.

Apart from the foregoing distinctions concerning short-term and long-term models and planning objectives, there is an important difference between the policy uses to which quantitative economic models are put in The Netherlands and those in France and Japan. The Netherlands Central Planning Bureau follows the Tinbergen approach, in which, it will be recalled, a policy model is derived from the complete structural model of the economy by eliminating the irrelevant endogenous variables. The equations of the policy model are then solved for the unknown instrument values which would achieve a specified set of target values under the forecasted economic conditions. If a conditional-maximization, preference-function approach were followed instead, the unknowns in the final set of policy equations would include the values of the flexible targets as well as those of the instruments. In either case, the fundamental purpose of the policy analysis is to use the econometric model, in combination with information about the decision-maker's preferences, to solve for an explicit set of quantitative governmental actions designed to achieve certain quantitatively specified policy objectives.

In contrast, the French and Japanese projections are used primarily to discover the physical and financial conditions which must be met if a certain growth rate is to be realized, rather than to design an explicit quantitative policy to achieve that objective. That is, from a planning point of view, the principal unknowns are the sectoral investment and production targets which are implied by, and consistent with, the macrostructure and input-output relationships of the economy and the exogenously specified rates of increase of labor input and GNP (or labor input and productivity) and exports. Once these investment and production targets are determined, their achievement is left largely to the private initiative of businessmen, modified or conditioned by the use of the financial and regulatory powers of the state. Such powers involve the use of policy instruments, of course, but the important point in the present context is that the decision regarding their use is not the subject of investigation within the economic model.

However, policy variables are not completely neglected in the long-term models. In the Japanese development model described by Shishido, for example, there are five policy parameters: the share of government purchases in GNP, the share of transfer payments in GNP, the indirect tax ratio on GNP, and the direct tax ratios on wage and nonwage income respectively. These last two tax ratios are treated endogenously, but the other ratios are exogenous. It is interesting to note also that the government surplus is treated as an exogenously fixed target, because of a traditional policy of adherence to a balanced budget. As Shishido shows, the model can be used to study the macroeconomic implications of quantitative variations in the exogenously given policy instruments, external conditions, and limiting factors. In this way, the model can be used to search for a consistent set of macroeconomic instruments and targets by successive approximations, and the approach is therefore akin in spirit to that of Tinbergen, although methodologically less direct than his. . . .

EFFECTIVENESS OF PLANNING TECHNIQUES

It is difficult to generalize about the influence of quantitative planning on either the economic policies or the economic experience of our small sample of countries. The closest link between quantitative economic analysis and actual policy decisions is clearly to be found in The Netherlands. There the short-term macroeconomic model is used not only to make forecasts on the assumption of unchanged policies but also to predict the policy outcomes associated with proposed action programs or to predict the instrumental combinations needed to achieve specified targets.

It is apparent from both papers on Dutch planning, moreover, that the quantitative estimates of the Central Planning Bureau do indeed importantly affect the actual decisions concerning wage and fiscal policies, although having less to do directly with monetary policy. Hessel points out, however, that the margin of action on wage and fiscal policies in 1957 and 1959 was smaller than the margin of unforeseen changes, in the sense that the predicted changes in important target variables (as a result of the policy actions taken) were smaller than the differences between the forecasts incorporating the policy actions and the actual performance of the economy. In similar vein, C. A. van den Beld notes that the procyclical fiscal and monetary actions of the early and mid-1950's are partly to be explained by forecasting errors. But he also notes improvement after 1958 in both the forecasts and the policy actions with regard to stabilization goals, and he stresses that some of the earlier destabilizing policy actions resulted partly from political considerations affecting the choice of target and instrument values. Finally, both authors allude briefly to the acute labor market tensions and large wage increases developing late in 1963, which highlight the difficulties of reconciling competing claims on the national income with the achievement of stable full employment growth without inflation.

As already mentioned, the French system of "indicative planning," although quantitative in character, is only indirectly concerned with specific governmental decisions about quantitative economic policy. Instead, its primary purpose is to estimate consistent four- or five-year quantitative growth targets for both the private and public sectors. As Cazes points out, the achievement of the planning goals is left largely to the phenomenon of "self-fulfilling prophecy," according to which "a belief is verified to the degree to which it is held by a sufficient number of people." This process is doubtless facilitated by the intricate network of government agencies and private commissions and working groups which is utilized in the preparation of each plan, since this institutional framework assures that the major decision-making groups participate closely in the determination of the plan's objectives. The result is that the objectives are probably more internally consistent than would otherwise be true and that the action groups are more favorably disposed psychologically to act on the basis of the plan.

Far from complete reliance, however, is placed on individual initiative to attain the goals of the plan. Again as mentioned earlier, the considerable financial and regulatory powers of the French government are used to reduce private deviations from the plan wherever possible. Moreover, although the plan does not represent a four-year budget in which the global allocation and the distribution of public expenditures are rigidly determined, the annual budgets are nevertheless articulated with the plans. Since public investment accounts for about one third of all fixed capital formation in France, the control of public expenditure in itself affords the government great leverage over the accomplishment of the plan's general objectives.

In Japan, as in France, the principal emphasis is on indicative planning for long-term growth, rather than on the quantitative analysis of short-term policy decisions. Neither of our writers on Japanese planning claims an intimate relationship between the formal quantitative projections and actual governmental policies, and Watanabe in particular expresses skepticism about the effectiveness of national quantitative planning insofar as actual economic performance is concerned. On a technical level, the quantitative projections have regularly underestimated actual performance and there appear to be serious internal inconsistencies in the present ten-year plan. Watanabe also stresses the smaller political influence of the Economic Planning Agency relative to that of other key government agencies — a situation which he believes has sometimes resulted in policy decisions inconsistent with the overall national plan. Finally, both Shishido and Watanabe refer to the failure to achieve a sufficient growth of social overhead capital, such as transportation, water, and sewage facilities. They attribute the shortage of such facilities to inadequate projections of the need, rather than to failure to implement the planned volume of public investment.

Needless to say, a balanced summary of the effectiveness of quantitative planning techniques in the various countries is difficult to encompass within a few brief paragraphs, and the reader is referred to the detailed appraisals offered in the papers themselves so that he may form his own impressions and judgments. I believe that enough has been said, however, to show that the authors are thoroughly aware of the weaknesses as well as the strengths of existing methods for the planning and implementation of quantitative economic policy. . . .

Thus, to conclude the volume with Charles C. Holt's reflections on the current status of and future need for research on various aspects of quantitative-decision analysis as it relates to national economic policy seems especially appropriate. He places particular stress on the need to develop quantitative knowledge about welfare objectives and their relative importance in the preference or social welfare function, since this is presently the area of greatest ignorance. He does not, however, neglect the search for better technical methods for handling the statistical decision problem under conditions of dynamic uncertainty or for improving the estimation of economic relations, and he concludes by distinguishing a fourth problem area of a less technical nature, though of equal or greater importance than the others. This is the problem of relating the professional advice of the economist to the political-decision process so that the economist's quantitative analysis may be of maximum effectiveness and use to the responsible decision-makers. In this connection, and also with regard to preferences, Holt stresses that the skills, techniques, and theory of other social science disciplines and the legal profession need to be brought to bear on problems which cannot be solved with the economist's tool kit alone.

RESEARCH SUGGESTIONS

Holt's paper provides a cogent basic agenda for the sort of multipronged attack that would be required for full development of the promise implicit in current techniques of quantitative-decision analysis. It may be useful to supplement his presentation with a brief summary of some of the research suggestions made in the other papers (and during the conference discussions), without attempting to establish priorities or implying that every conferee would agree with every suggestion.

With regard to the preference function, agreement was general on the great importance of quantifying welfare objectives and the trade-offs between them. One line of approach would be quantitative studies of the welfare losses corresponding to different degrees of unemployment, inflation, rates of economic growth, and other major policy goals. The purpose would be to provide a more objective basis for the formulation of social value judgments about policy targets and instruments. Other suggestions concerned the direct collection of data on preferences, as by questionnaires and interviews, and the inference of revealed preferences of policy-makers from empirical analysis of their actual decisions. Isolated examples of all these approaches can be found in the literature, but the area has nevertheless been comparatively neglected and deserves much more systematic attention than economists have given it to date.

Another profitable line of investigation is to find the sensitivity of the optimal policy solutions for a given economic model to different types of preference functions. If the optimal solutions are rather sensitive to small variations in the weights or form of the preference function, the decision-maker could be presented with several alternative solutions derived under different preference assumptions and could choose among them on the basis of his evaluation of the preferences. An example of an experimental sensitivity analysis is given in Theil's paper.

Research on the preference function may encounter some knotty identification problems in realistic situations. One difficulty is that preferences, while in principle independent of the constraints expressed in the economic model, may in practice be related to them. That is, the interpretation placed on the constraints, and the uncertainty discounts attached to them, may be influenced by the policy-maker's preferences. Conversely, his preferences may be influenced by what is thought possible of achievement under the constraints; hence the preferences may change as the constraints do. Indeed, this is virtually certain to happen (or appear to happen) if only a few policy objectives are made explicit at a given time, as is amply demonstrated in the historical examples given in the country papers of shifts in the principal targets in response to the changing economic situation. Such observed changes may represent a movement to a new position along a stable preference function, but in practice it may be impossible to distinguish such movements from shifts to new preference functions.

Another kind of interdependence is to be found in committee situations where there is bargaining over the weights to be attached to the variables in a collective preference function. Individual preferences may be deliberately misrepresented to establish bargaining positions, and stated preferences may therefore depend on estimates of the likely positions to be taken by other participants and of their "true" preferences. In general, the sociological, group-dynamic, and game-theoretic aspects of the administrative interactions involved in the determination of policy objectives, are indicative of important problems for theoretical and empirical research in an essentially interdisciplinary field.

With regard to model building, the problems of better specification of structural relationships and of improvements in statistical data received the bulk of attention at the conference, partly because so much progress has already occurred in the development of refined techniques of parameter estimation. The most obvious, but albeit also the most important, suggestion of this character is that explicit attention be given to policy problems in future attempts to improve econometric models. Models without explicit policy variables and parameters may be of some use for forecasting purposes, but to be of real assistance in decision-making, a model must include relevant instrumental variables.

This precept has been kept at the forefront, incidentally, in the quarterly econometric model of the United States economy which was constructed by an interuniversity team under the sponsorship of the Social Science Research Council Committee on Economic Stability. This model, which is now undergoing further development and testing at the Brookings Institution under the supervision of Lawrence R. Klein and Gary Fromm, includes many more governmental and financial equations than have previous efforts of this type and offers great promise for investigation and simulation of the effects of quantitative fiscal and monetary policies on economic stability.[4] In view of the substantial importance attached to the instruments of monetary policy in all Western countries (see the paper by Kirschen and Morissens), the monetary sectors of most econometric models appear surprisingly rudimentary, even after allowing for the inherent difficulties of establishing the relevant relationships within financial markets and between financial and real variables.

With the increasing attention being devoted to growth problems even in industrialized countries, further development of econometric growth models may confidently be expected. Thus Cazes reports that, to provide the basic framework for parliamentary debate on the Fifth Plan, the French are using a global econometric model in which the growth rate of GNP is an endogenous variable dependent on specific assumptions about resource development and productivity change, in sharp contrast to the methods and assumptions employed in the earlier plans. The Japanese are also experimenting with long-term models taking explicit account of technical progress and capital-labor substitution, and capable of projecting the intermediate paths to be taken by a limited number of basic indicators throughout the ten-year plan-

---

[4] The Brookings-SSRC model is briefly discussed in the Fox-Thorbecke paper. For further details, see *The Brookings-SSRC Quarterly Econometric Model of the United States,* edited by James S. Duesenberry, Gary Fromm, Lawrence R. Klein, and Edwin Kuh, which is scheduled for publication by Rand McNally (Chicago) and North-Holland (Amsterdam) in early 1965.

ning period (see the paper by Shishido). Similar work is now underway in United States academic circles.

It is still uncertain how closely short-term and long-term models can be integrated. Quarterly or even monthly models may be necessary for full understanding of the business cycle and for purposes of short term forecasting and the planning of stabilization policy, and they offer the further advantage of reducing simultaneous structural interdependence, with its attendant difficulties of estimation and causal interpretation (see the Fox-Thorbecke and Sengupta papers). Such models must necessarily emphasize short-term decisions and relationships which are inconsequential for long-term development, however. It is probable that for some time to come it will be necessary to maintain separate models for different purposes, as in the Japanese scheme of a quarterly (or annual) short-term model, a long-term (5-10-year) model, and a perspective (10-20-year) model. All the same, the links among such models will doubtless be strengthened by the elaboration of production functions and the inclusion of endogenous variations in the capital stock and the labor force.

CONCLUSION

There is no doubt that planning is a growth industry. It has become legitimized where previously suspect and has had some success where tried. In a word, it is now respectable. But as the first blush of enthusiasm gives way to sober consideration of sticky problems, the practical issues of refinement and implementation take precedence. There is room for many great debates: the technician versus the politician; theoretical elegance versus empirical rough-and-readiness; centralization versus decentralization; incentives versus degrees and kinds of coercion; rules versus authority. These cannot be resolved on a universal level; the bill of particulars is too important. We should be thankful for such diversity and experimentation. Countries have much to learn from each other, and competition among systems should lead to efficient selection and combination. The articles in this volume were chosen to emphasize this variety and diversity. The emphasis has been on interpretive essays to illuminate the lively issues surrounding planning.

If diversity is the keynote, controversy is the mood. Discussion of planning engages man's heart as well as his mind. A quintessential problem in analyzing planning has been that at its very core are great moral and political issues, and thus it can never be judged solely on technical considerations. Like other all-encompassing concerns, the discussion of planning impinges on sensitive and troubled areas. The problems are always multidimensional.

But behind the controversies, technical and otherwise, the forces of convergence are slowly taking hold. Economies which seem different in all important respects—stage of development, ideological orientation, economic structure—are evolving toward the use of broadly similar methods to govern their resource allocation decisions. Partly this reflects processes of choice and adaptation, the transfer of technique and knowledge, and the emulation of successful experimentation. Partly, it is a result of the relentless march of technology and the organizational imperatives that follow, albeit often with a disturbing lag, in its wake.

We must not minimize some very important and substantive differences which will continue for a long time; the operative word is "evolving." Nor should it be suggested that the future will emerge as a pale carbon-copy of this or that system now existing. The point is that there will be much borrowing, mutating, sloughing off, and innovating by all; economies will undergo a process analogous to selective absorption. The future is likely to reverse our present modes of thought. Today we emphasize the differences among nations in their economic policies, although we recognize some similarities. The common basis of planning, no matter what formal differences persist, will compel us to adopt a new perspective.

SUGGESTIONS FOR READING

For a survey of the classical discussion of the possibility and rationality of planning, see the review article by A. Bergson, "Socialist Economics" in *Survey of Contemporary Economics*, Vol. I, edited by H. S. Ellis (Homewood, Ill., 1948). On methods and techniques of planning, the following can be read with profit: J. Tinbergen, *Central Planning* (New Haven); R. Radner, *Notes on the Theory of Economic Planning;* R. Solow, "Some Problems of the Theory and Practice of Economic Planning," *Economic Development and Cultural Change*, Jan. 1962; H. Chenery, "Development Policies and Progammes," *Economic Bulletin for Latin America*, Vol. III (1958); R. Eckaus, "Appendix on Development Planning," in C. P. Kindleberger, *Economic Development*, 2nd edition (New York, 1965); and D. Seers, "Economic Programming," *Social and Economic Studies,* March 1962.

On Western planning, see: J. Dow, *The Management of the British Economy* (New York, 1963); *Economic Planning in a Democratic Society*, ed. T. Reid (Toronto, 1963); V. Bassie, "Economic Planning in Western Europe," *Quarterly Review of Economics and Business,* Summer 1963; P. Masse, "French Methods of Planning," *Journal of Industrial Economics,* Nov. 1962; W. Blass, "Economic Planning, European Style," *Harvard Business Review,* Sept.–Oct. 1963; and C. Pratten, "The Best-Laid Plans . . . ," *Lloyds Bank Review,* July 1964.

For planning in Soviet-area countries, it will be useful to consult the following: G. Grossman, "Notes for a Theory of the Command Economy," *Soviet Studies,* Oct. 1963; N. Spulber, "Contrasting Economic Patterns: Chinese and Soviet Development Strategies," *Soviet Studies,* July 1963; H. Hunter, "Optimum Tautness in Developmental Planning," *Economic Development and Cultural Change,* July 1961; J. Stanovnik, "Planning through the Market," *Foreign Affairs,* Jan. 1962; M. Kaser, "The Nature of Soviet Planning," *Soviet Studies,* Oct. 1962; and J. M. Montias, *Central Planning in Poland* (New Haven, 1962).

Literature on planning in the developing areas is growing rapidly. A representative list would include the following: A. Watson and J. Dirlan, "The Impact of Underdevelopment on Economic Planning," *Quarterly Journal of Economics,* May 1965; "Planning in Latin America," *Economic Bulletin for Latin America,* 1963; D. R. Gadgil, *Planning and Economic Policy in India* (Bombay, India); B. Cameron, "On Development Planning," *International Economic Review,* Jan. 1964; C. Wilcox, *The Planning and Execution of Economic Development in Southeast Asia;* R. Green, "Four African Development Plans," *Journal of Modern African Studies,* Vol. III (1965); and *Leading Issues in Development Economics,* ed. G. M. Meier (New York, 1964), Chapters VIII and IX.